Dedicated to
—Our Youth

The Scent of Love

Patricia Liu

BOOKLOVER INTERNATIONAL CULTURE PRESS
AN IMPRINT OF METRO FIFTH AVENUE PRESS,LLC

The Scent of Love

ISBN 978-1626090-24-8

Printed in the United States of America

Abstract

The Scent of Love is a book based on dairies written in college. A detailed account of almost day-to-day life from 1997 to 2001, records many aspects of a Chinese student's college life. The year 1997 saw the beginning of the nation-wide paid college education. Tuition fees became a big burden for millions of rural families. To be a college student was not a personal thing of any one individual. The whole village might contribute to the cultivation of one talent. Thus, this book firstly is a tribute to the kindness and generosity of farmers, whose help made it possible for the author to continue her study in college.

Patricia Liu went to the big city Zhengzhou to start a life-long romance with English. Her struggle in learning the language and understanding the western culture is another metamorphosis of college life. English has become a must in earning many degrees since the late 1990s. The battle was fought not only over grammars, vocabularies and pronunciations, but more deeply over two very conflicting logics and mentalities. Thus, the second wish for this book is that it can celebrate the hard work of a generation in their studying of English. Such nation-wide English campaign has paved the way for a better understanding of the world beyond China.

And, yes, love!

Patricia is a romantic, like all of us. In China, the leashes around the necks of teenagers are loosened in college. Students in relationships are not punished by the school authority or frowned upon by protective parents any more. "To fall in love" is informally permitted, finally. The many misunderstandings, misfortunes and mistakes are the miscarried children of suppressed illusions about romances. The love that they loved in college is a mixture of loves for boys, girls, birds, flowers, strangers and friends. It is the love in which they create a new self in the embrace of transient happiness and long-lasting sorrows. Thus, it explains the name of and the final purpose of the book.

The Scent of Love is structured by chapters. The college life in China oscillates from summer vacations to winter vacations and from school life in the city to family life in the countryside. Each school year contains four terms. Each chapter is a term. The form of dairies is maintained to preserve the original flavor of the first-hand intensity.

When English is used to weave a Chinese dream, a deep chord is struck between the oriental and the occidental. Read the stories and touch the tender heart of a real China.

Preface

We've all been there. We've all been young and eager and silly. Let's recall it, sing it, and smell the scent of it. Let's connect: East and West, past and present, city and country, tradition and modern...

We've all been there. Again, let's drink from the fountain of love and make our pilgrimage to a time called YOUTH.

After my nineteenth's birthday I went to Zhengzhou University and started a life of the best and the worst. I came to the city on a train and left it on another train. I stopped there for four years and then moved on. Like so many others I've pushed and been pushed here and there in a changing China; I've swirled around the wheel of destiny with the swirling destiny of the country; I've looked South and North, East and West but have found nothing to hold on. Then, I turn 30. When my college students call me "mum" I know it's time to take a break, to look back for a while, to recharge my wavering beliefs with love and dreams, and to tell you when it is still raw.

Share with me, dear you, my love and my dream in the best and worst period of the life, called college.

c o n t e n t

Chapter Nine

Chapter Ten

Chapter Eleven

Chapter Twelve

Chapter Thirteen

Chapter Fourteen

Chapter Fifteen

Chapter One

Not all Kisses are Love

August 28

I am in a train for Zhengzhou now. Brother insisted on accompanying me. He worried that I would be cheated and sold by some "bad eggs", as was popularly feared in the village.[1] He must accompany me on the first trip.

We took train from Lingbao Station. It was strange that I should run into my "little prince" there. Just as we were about to get on the train he showed up, smiled to me and wished me good luck. Did he know I was leaving or did he just happen to be there? Anyhow with the goodbye from a boy cherished in my dream my leaving was complete and official. He and I are impossible. I need to move on. He wishes me to move on.

It's 7 p.m. now. Night has come. Brother and I each have eaten two boiled eggs we brought. The train is a slow one and stops at every small station. Passengers are falling asleep one by

---

[1] It used to be rumored that girls would be kidnapped and married into the mountainous regions when they traveled alone.

one. There are no seats for us. Brother sits on my trunk and I sit on a bundle of quilts.

He is like a faithful bodyguard. He never yawns. His eyes are wide open, guarding the 6,000 Yuan in the trunk and his little sister. I feel safe.

It's getting darker and darker outside. Will the legendary robbers come? It's rumored in the village that every train is "taken care of" by a gang with names such as Tiger, Haohan (good man), and Wild Wolf etc. They would blow a kind of powder into the air and take the money from passengers who fell asleep on sniffing the poisonous smoke. Their tricks are quite old. Maybe they took it after the 108 LiangShanHaohan from one of the four classics *Outlaws of the Marsh*. It is a book on the peasant rebellion in Song Dynasty, a dynasty of great separation of the middle kingdom in the 11th and 12th century. In defiance of local and central tyranny the 108 outcasts gathered together in mountain Liang (Liangshan). They had marvelous Kong fu and they robbed the rich to give the poor. They are the Chinese version of Robin Hood and his knights. Only unlike the 108 "good man", the robbers on the train robbed anyone asleep and I doubt very much that they would give the money to the poor. No one, not even police can do anything about it.

I feel drowsy now. Oh my goodness, they are coming! A fat man walks into the compartment with a knife! And, he is searching the pockets of sleeping passengers! He is followed by four strong men with snarling faces. Those who are still awake stare at the gangs nervously. No one is doing anything about it, including a woman assistant who walked away just minutes before the gangs came. Should I do something? What should I do?

...

They are leaving for another box now. The gang walk quickly along the aisle, ignore those with open eyes, search those who were asleep, take money and watches as if picking up their own stuff and leave for the next box quickly. I am appalled by their expertise. They didn't even look at me. My notebook, pen or even the bundle I sit on did not attract them at all. Brother stared at the men when they passed me. He was ready to do anything if they touched me. They totally ignored me and moved on. Brother sat firmly on our trunk. He was not searched. Once they leave, the box becomes alive. Some people go frantic, some go bankrupt, and some become very excited. They all have some gossip for home now. They have come out to "see the world" in good ways and bad ways. I don't feel good. What if my brother is not with me? Who am I going to trust in a world no one cares about others anymore? What will college life be like? I am tired. Brother is urging me to get some sleep.

Good night, the world.

August 29

First day at college!

I am alone in Room 202 now, recording my first day in college.

We arrived at the Zhengzhou station in the early morning. The broadcast in the train said Zhengzhou station is the biggest transitional station in Asia. I am not sure. It is really crowded but not that big.

Students from the college were waiting. They wore a red band around their arms. On the band was written the name of Zhengzhou University. They looked very nice. My anxiety was eased a little. They helped us onto a school bus. We arrived at the university in about 20 minutes. The city looked clean and spacious. The campus was pretty. I really felt good when the school bus drove leisurely on the wide road lined with parasol trees.

A girl led brother and I to my dorm—Room 202 in Building 8. It was a small room, smaller than my room back at home. There were 4 bunk beds. I found my name on a lower bunk near the door. A girl was packing on the bed above mine. She said " 来啦 " (there you are) to me and busied in her bed. Brother helped me unpack, cleaned my bed, put a quilt on it and went to buy toilet articles for me. He bought me a red basin, a pink cup, a bar of soap and a green towel.

Then we went to " 报　到 "— check in officially. I needed to check in at 12 different units—the personnel, the library, the clinic, the financial unit, the English department etc. I needed to collect 12 stamps and then went to sign my name on a list named Class one, Grade one the first semester of 1997-1998. Brother was with me all the time. We did not talk much. He watched me protectively while I stood in one long queue after another. I was excited, nervous and upset at the same time. So many emotions choked me that I did not have any appetite when brother bought a piece of bread for me. It was 4pm. There were still two stamps to be banged in my check-in list. Brother looked dry and piteous.

I insisted to share the bread with him. He refused. He said he already had one. I knew he lied. By 5 p.m. I was officially a college student in Zhengzhou University, the best university in Henan province, central China. Brother needed to go back home. I walked with him to a bank near the north gate of the school. He deposited the remaining 500 Yuan in my name, my allowance for this semester. His stern face broke into a tiny smile when he asked the bank assistant to "take care of my little sister". He said this to the teachers and the girls in my dorm. Then he took Trolley 102 that runs by the north gate and left. I was totally alone in the city. The north gate looked nostalgia and forlorn in the setting sun. Bye-bye, 哥哥! How am I going to survive the four college years?

August 30

There is still one bed empty in my dorm. Maybe she hasn't borrowed enough money to pay the tuition. Poor girl! Will she ever show up?

August 31

She came last night. Her big eyes shine brightly on her fair face. I like her instantly. She comes the last but has the loudest voice. Now, she is ordering us to put things in order. I must stop writing.

September 1

College life starts from Room 202. We have found out each

other's age, birthday and home town. A hierarchy based on age was built up quickly. I am No. 2, the second oldest girl among the eight. The one with big eyes and loud voice is No. 6. There are five horses, one sheep and two monkeys in our dorm.[2] One of the monkeys is from my town in the western part of the province. The other six girls are all from eastern or central part of the province. Me and my monkey speak our local dialect while the other girls speak the notorious Henan dialect. Eight sisters! Can we live happily hereafter?

September 5

The fourth day of one month's military training.

A girl fainted while we were standing erect in the hot sun. Good for her! I envied her when she was sent to the school clinic.

September 15

I miss home. I am so lonely. College is boring.

I cried when the school broadcast sang a song of *"we are the soldiers"*.

We, the soldiers, are not so different

We, too, have mothers and fathers

We, too, miss our hometown…

I sobbed when we were assembling for a goodnight slogan. The officer would say: comrades, you've worked hard. The

---

2 This is a Chinese way to remember a person's year of birth. There are twelve animals: mouse, cow, tiger, rabbit, dragon, snake, horse, sheep, monkey, rooster, dog, pig. These animals each represent a year. People usually get to know each other's age by the animal year they were born.

student soldiers would reply: To serve the people. I opened my mouth and cried loud. I felt so lonely—strange city, strange people, strange dialect, unfriendly roommates. How I missed my family, my friends, and my little prince! I cried loud and was quickly followed by more sobs from other "soldiers". The young officer was surprised at his tearful comrades. He dispersed his army quickly.

September 20

Clinton (an old friend from high school) came to see me this noon. He called when I was having cold noodle as lunch. He waited for me in the rose garden. I was a little shy when he observed me carefully and said I looked beautiful in the green uniform. He had a gift for me. It was a set of *Crazy English*, a book with two tapes. I opened the book after he left. There were two sentences on the first page: Whatever you do, wherever you go, I will be right here waiting for you and his large signature. My heart warmed at the words. The melody of the old song *Right here waiting* rang in my mind.

September25

A long and exhausting day.

The troops marched to the wild for field training today. The young officer called me a coward. I couldn't even hold the gun steadily over my shoulder. I closed my eyes when he became impatient and shot the bullet for me. I was annoyed at being a coward and asked for another try. No. Every soldier had only one bullet. I missed my chance and became a coward for the military training. Fortunately I was only one of the cowards. Many girls who could walk the "square steps" beautifully refused to touch a gun.[3] The military training ended at last. Strangely, like many other girls I've grown attached to the young officer. He is the one who introduced us to our college life. What gift can we give him? We are discussing it in the dorm now.

September 27

A day of farewell.

A big bus took the officers back to their real troops. Their student soldiers held their hands through the windows and wouldn't let go. The bus moved slowly through the tearful girls. I thrust a big white handkerchief to the young officer with the names of the eight girls stitched on it. His eyes were red. Goodbye, dear officers. Thank you for the drills in the sun, for the military songs, for the heroic stories, and for being with us for the first phase of college life. By the way, I am not a coward.

September28

School starts today. The girls in room 202 are allotted in the same class. We are roommates and classmates now and I am appointed monitor of study by the instructor. Maybe the stunning score of English for the college entrance exam has earned me this position. I had the highest score in my district.

---

3 "Square steps" are the steps a soldier take on a formal march. He walks with his arms across his body like a square.

I am eager for learning. I've finished the *Crazy English* given by Clinton. It's a good book. It contains everything: news, poems, songs, movie scripts, interviews etc. and the original sound. I hear Madonna's voice for the first time. She talks about her tour and her missing her mum. Poor girl, her mother died when she was only five years old. I don't know much about her but I like her for her courage. In a peculiar way I link her with the spirit of her country. What is America like? Maybe I can go for a visit someday.

October16

The only class I like is oral English. Patrick is from the US. He is the first foreigner I have ever seen. He looks so handsome. He has curly golden hair, white-pink skin and a very high nose. He speaks slowly so that we can catch up with him.

Yesterday he gave each of his us an English name. Mine is Patricia. Patrick explained that it meant noble and capable of great love. Mmmm, good name. Capable of great love? I think so. Youth is stirring in my heart. I am secretly ready for love. Alas, there are only five boys in my class. Who can " 谈恋爱 "—"talk about love" with me? Clinton is in another university in the suburb of Zhengzhou. Too far. I need someone around me. Besides, I used to dislike him a lot in high school when he kept running and running in the playground after he failed the 3,000meters in the sports meeting. To "talk about love" with someone like him is too serious to be fun. What about the boys in my class? Let me think. One is too short, one is almost bald, one has a bad smell, one has a baby face and the last one, the monitor has a big tongue. No one is qualified.

Go to the library then. I need to read original English books. I need to keep my edge and run ahead of others.

October19

Autumn has come. It's getting quite cool these days. Monitor and I went shopping for a curtain for our classroom this morning. He asked me whether I had a boyfriend. He said he just broke up with his girlfriend. He looked me steadily into my eyes when he talked. I was a little off guard. I told him I did not have a boyfriend. Then he held my hand when we crossed the street. What is happening?

The blue velvet curtain looks pretty on the spacious windows.

October25

Monitor calls me frequently these days. He says he has class business to discuss with me. I am a little confused now. Does he want to "talk about love" with me? How should I conduct myself? Should I refuse when he holds my hand again? Well, there was a sense of pleasure when he held my hand several days ago. What should I do? The phone is ringing…

It was monitor. We met in the classroom, just he and I. I was nervous when he held my hand again. He said he could tell my fortune from palm reading. A lame excuse. I did not withdraw my hand. I pretended to be generous while my heart was pounding excitedly. He rubbed my fat short hand in his thin long hands and kissed my lips. I didn't even know how to kiss. I didn't open my mouth. With this first kiss on my lips I went back to the dorm in a trance. What am I doing? I have a boyfriend now. Is monitor my boyfriend?

October 27

How confusing! What should I do? Do I like him? Do I like staying with him all the time? He seems so experienced. He asked me for a walk yesterday afternoon along the man-made Golden River that runs through the campus and kissed me again. He told me his hometown, his family and his ex girlfriend. The girl bought him a tape recorder as a birthday present before they broke up. Now she was asking for 200 Yuan compensation. Monitor asked me whether he should pay back the money. I did not know. I told him if he wanted to pay her back I could lend him 200 Yuan by the end of the month. I am a governess now. I can earn some money. His thin long eyes sparkled and he kissed me again.

October 30

My roommates become hostile to me suddenly. They answer Monitor's phone gently but give me a cold face when he asks for me. What's wrong? Am I a bad girl because I have a boyfriend? Come on, girls, we are college students!

November 3

I had the first salary yesterday, 250 Yuan for tutoring a high school boy for a month. I lent 200 Yuan to Monitor. I quite like him now. I want him to pay back his debt and be over with his ex.

November9

What a waste of time! I did not know "talking about love" could be so time-consuming. I did not have a single nap last week. Monitor called me after every lunch and then we talked and kissed in the empty classroom. And we had the lovers' walk by the golden river every night. I begin to worry about my study now.

The eight girls are on two sides now. No. 4 and No. 7 are on my side. We are emotional and scream easily. We eat together and go to the classroom together. No. 4 is my pet. She looks as vulnerable as Lin Daiyu from *A Dream of the Red Mansions*. It is the best of the four classics. It is written by Cao Xueqin in Qing Dynasty. Daiyu, the orphan girl transformed from a crying grass loves her cousin Baoyu who marries another cousin named Baochai in the end. Daiyu, who cries even at the falling petals sheds her last tear for Baoyu, dies on his wedding day and turns into a grass. It's a most tragic love story and Daiyu has since become the symbol of gentle beauty. No. 4 is as piteous and gentle as Daiyu. She follows me around like a little sister. I don't mind washing her bowl at all. No. 7 is from my home town. The same dialect draws us together. On the other side are the left five girls. No. 6 used to be close to me. She stopped smiling at me when I screamed and danced and did not behave myself as "a traditional farmer's girl should". She is the head of her side. There has been a cold war between us since I "fooled around" with monitor. What can I do about it? It's so troublesome to have a boyfriend.

November12

I did a bad thing today, a really bad thing. I still feel stupid now.

We had oral English in the morning. Patrick came with his mother. He introduced the old lady to the class and said we could ask her questions. No one dared to ask. We all sat there as still as statues.

"Any questions? You may ask my mother any questions. Don't be shy." Patrick encouraged us. Still no questions. I felt uneasy. As the monitor of study I thought maybe I should ask the first question. I stood up: "How old are you?" Before I could finish my question Patrick broke in sharply: "Patricia, it is rude. You never ask a lady her age. Sit down!" I was mortified. Me? Rude? How? I was just trying to be nice. I sank into my seat, my face burning. O, you hypocritea! What do you mean by "any question"? What's wrong with one of the most common questions in China? What's wrong about asking someone's age? Don't you have an age? I thought furiously and hated the lady who stood at the platform with knotted brows.

I have to admit that language learning is not perfect if you can't cross the cultural barriers. I still remember Patrick's surprised face when I told him I was on my way to teach English at a certain place. I should have known better. A simple "hi" would suffice. I shouldn't have followed the Chinese way of thinking and told him where I was going. It's my *"privacy"*. Yet, it is just hard for me to hide my privacy if it contains my age, my food or the places I am going. Are we really so different? Ah, headache! Go to bed, then.

November15

I told monitor that we should spend more time studying English instead of fooling around. He agreed but went to a movie without me. He is not interested in English. English scares him. He makes simple grammar mistakes, pronounces poorly and gets very upset.

It's getting really cold now. No. 3 is knitting a scarf for a potential boyfriend in Tibet. It's touching to see the hot-tempered girl sitting quietly in her bed knitting. Maybe I can knit one for monitor.

November 16

Look, Patricia Liu is knitting, too. I feel like a woman for the first time in my life. I am knitting a white scarf for monitor. Where is he, by the way? He is cold to me after I told him to spend more time on English. Stupid boy!

November19

Monitor called, not for me but for No. 4. I was shocked. It was the third time he called for No. 4. What's going on?

November21

Another night was wasted. I went to the city square with monitor. He said spending time together with No. 4 was a way to show his love for me. No. 4 was my closest friend. He felt close to me when they hang around. All they talked about was me. What should I say to such an explanation? Maybe he could hang around with others when I couldn't spend some time for him. He needs company in his healing phase from his ex. We had dinner together in a small restaurant. I felt clumsy when he fed me with his chopsticks. What's the point? I could feed myself perfectly. Then we cuddled in the rose garden. He talked high tonight. He talked of marriage, family, and *our baby*—all beyond my comprehension. Then suddenly he touched my breast and squeezed. I was taken aback. This is a bad move. This is dirty. I thought frantically in my mind but a sense of strong pleasure seized me. He whispered "let's make love tonight" and kissed me hard. Make love? Impossible! I pushed him away and told him I was not ready yet. What's wrong with him? Why does he want to do such a dirty thing? Didn't Confucius say "lust is the first evil"? I don't even want to think about it now! He said it was ok. He could wait. I could see disappointment in his long eyes. What should I do?

November 25

Reading letters from old friends is more enjoyable than fooling around with monitor. Pretty, my best friend from high school is studying in a college in Kaifeng, the old capital of Northern Song Dynasty; Yingzi, another friend from high school is studying in a technical institute in Zhengzhou; Po, an old friend since junior high school is in the same college with Yingzi; Rui, my dear friend from high school is in the same college with Clinton. Their letters would come every Friday. I feel so rich and so loved when reading their letters.

It's getting cold. I finished the scarf this afternoon and put it around monitor's neck when we were sitting in the rose garden tonight. I hope he can feel my way of love.

November30

Ben is one of the five boys in my class. He studies really hard. He is always reading and writing in the classroom. I admire him. He has such strength in him. He knows what he wants and he goes for it. He wants the first scholarship. He is from one of the poorest counties of the province. He eats the left –over in the school cafeteria. He tells me this without any embarrassment. Every time I talk with him I feel small. I am no better off than him. I need the scholarship, too. Why can't I study as hard as he does? Monitor has a bad influence on me. I must keep clear-headed and study hard. Final exam is drawing near. It's no joke.

December 4

I hate myself. I just can't concentrate! The two empty seats of monitor and No.4 are bothering me. He is away at the cinema with my friend and the white scarf. Is No. 4 still my friend? I am sick of pretending. We've stopped eating together. My side is dispersing.

No. 6 said I was a fool yesterday. I nursed a snake in my own bosom. Maybe she is right. What is he doing now, kissing No.4, squeezing her breasts or making love? O, I am so sick. I can't write anymore.

December 9

Monitor asked me out again. He did not answer me when I asked about the relations between him and No. 4. He just led me into a dark classroom and kissed me. Then his hands went down my body and tried to take off my pants. What the hell was he doing? My blood went cold. I was disgusted with him there and then. I stayed with him in the classroom the whole night, no talking, nor love making. I was too perplexed even to think. Maybe I should let him go. He is not my type. I went back to my dorm, empty and depressed. No. 4 was crying. I am tired, really tired.

December14

Thank God, there is a letter from Clinton. How I want his brotherly care now! How I need to talk with a righteous and healthy man like Clinton! I wrote him a long letter and told him about monitor. What will he say? Will he "talk about love" with me?

December20

Clinton be hanged! He said he did not have time to care about a girl who was "not pure" any more. You arrogant fool! I tore his letter into pieces and shut him in the blacklist of my memory.

Snow is falling, the first snow since I came to the city. Pure white snow, am I not pure anymore? How so?

December21

It's bitingly cold. There is no heat in the classroom or in the dorm. Many students have caught flu. The school authority has offered each classroom a stove, a pot and a bottle of vinegar. It's the simplest way to prevent the spread of flu. We have our classes in the air of boiling vinegar.

I bought a thick red jacket. Monitor still wears the white scarf I knitted for him though we hardly talk now.

Poor Ben is coughing badly. Last night he wrapped the blue velvet curtain around his shaking body and stuffed newspapers in his broken shoes. I feel really sorry for him. We must do something for Ben.

December24

Christmas is coming. Our class has two gifts for Ben. One is a thick cotton coat and the other is a pair of thick fake leather shoes. Every student of our class donated 10 Yuan. I went shopping for Ben with a kind-hearted girl named Ying. We bought the coat and shoes with the 300 Yuan. I am not sure how we could give the gifts to Ben without hurting his pride.

December25

Merry Christmas, Patrick! Merry Christmas, the world! Merry Christmas, Ben!

Ben accepted the gifts on one condition. He could call me his little sister and I could call him my big brother from then on. Ok, it's a deal. Thank you, my kind classmates. We are all brothers and sisters, except monitor and No. 4. I am so confused. What kind of person is this monitor? What kind of person is No.4? Monitor complained to me once that I was too naive and not romantic enough. Then why don't you help me grow up? No.4, do you not see the pain in me? Are you not my friend? This is all too much for my "naive" mind. I need to concentrate on the coming exams.

January 5, 1998

We will have the first exam on Intensive Reading tomorrow. Monitor came up to me this evening and asked me to let him copy my answers tomorrow. Should I let him do this? I miss his kisses.

January10

Poor me, I betrayed my conscience and let him cheat in the exams. Then he went out with No. 4. I am such a big fool. I am disgusted at myself.

January18

The exams were finally over yesterday. All students are packing to go home. Monitor left this morning. I knew it from his call to No. 4. I lied in bed, totally awake. I thought of seeing him off. No, that is unnecessary. I touch my lips, gone are my first kisses.

January 19

It's snowing so hard.

I danced in the snow to the tune of *Tennessee Waltz*:

…

Now I know how much I have lost

I've lost my little darling…

Thus the first semester of the first school year in college ends, not with a laugh but with a big snow to a sad tune. I will go home today.

Chapter Two

Here and There

January20

I am home now. I've been thinking of Monitor all the time. I touched my lips and was puzzled. Why did he do that? My first kiss was thus given, with no good reason. Can I find out the reason in this winter vacation?

January 28

The Spring Festival is coming soon. The rooms would be decorated with new pictures. When I was tearing down the old ones I thought of Monitor. Love becomes a kind of hurt. I must keep silent about the story happened between us and regard it as something natural. Sometimes I'm a person who just destroys things. Clinton had real trust in me. He wanted to love me and to make me his dream girl but I just acted like a bad-tempered tigress. He was frightened and said I had changed too much to deserve his love. Well, life is a joke played on everybody especially those who want to enjoy it with his own characteristics.

Tomorrow is the last day of the old year. I must behave like a good daughter.

All the best to my friends!

December 29, 1997 (lunar calendar)

First let me wish all the people who love me a very happy new year!

I always wake up at midnight. I lie in bed thinking about the college life especially the story of the first love. I don't believe the existence of a false love, for love comes from heart. How can heart be false? Monitor has destroyed my dream of a perfect love and has drawn me down to the earth from the fairyland of imagination. I have helped him do this but it is Clinton who has been hurt, for his dream girl is no more there. Every time I think of the past and Monitor's coldness when we parted I am scared to care him anymore. I begin to doubt whether he has been playing a game with me all the time. I don't know what to do to recover my complete belief in love.

This afternoon when we were making Jiaozi, Mother told me a match-maker had come to propose a marriage for me with a boy named Po. My parents were in favor of this because it is so hard for them to support my education anymore. It's not a joke. At her words all my romantic feelings went away. I don't know whether Po loves me or not but I'm sure I don't love him. We are talking about marriage without love! This is too much for me. My God, what can I do? I need time to think about it.

What I need is not marriage but love. Can you give me that,

Po? Po and I were school mates in middle school. I don't know much about him. Why should he jump into my messy world? Anyhow he has reminded me of some old friends in middle school. I miss them and wish them all a happy Chinese New Year.

Be serious! Love is not a plaything!

I've made up my mind to support myself by being a governess. If I can be successful in this way I would refuse to be engaged to Po. I don't want a marriage without love.

January 3

Last night I cried and thought hard about my situation. To my surprise I thought of my "little prince" as the person that I would get engaged to. He had been my secret love from childhood. We used to be neighbors but now his family is so well-off that they have moved to a tall building on the other end of the village.

I'm tired now. How much I want to escape! Maybe the only way for me to take is to think of nothing. Just be happy. Life is so pure and absolute.

January 3

It's almost 11 p.m. I just came back from Ping's. Qin, Ping and I are childhood playmates. We had a chat at Ping's. I find that all of them are more realistic than me. They said all I had were dreams. I couldn't put dreams to use. They insisted that people didn't have true feelings for each other and I was too naive. I hate to live with a mask. Life would be so piteous without true things. I have been told again and again that I am naive. Now I think it is because I have faith in life. I also want to know the world outside my hometown in the countryside and the world outside China.

January 5

Though I've known for a long time that study is what I really want, it is now that I know how much I love studying. Every time I feel like destroying things, I would open a book to find light, dream and confidence. Today was strange day. I was worried about what I could do when I tiredly got up from bed. I planned to go dancing with Ping and Qin for the last night because tomorrow they would go back to their work in the city. However, I went to see a friend who is a doctor in the village. We had a chat from which I found I was such a small potato at my hometown where there were so many successful people especially females. Then I regretted the time wasted on being angry and hurt by petty things. Her father said that we should never give up trying and should make progress without stopping. I must think about my life rules. I find doing what I want to do is not always right because sometimes it is bad for my virtues and it draws me to the road which is farther and farther away from my dream.

What I need urgently is study. Without the ability trained from studying I would be a person of no value, no future and no root. Don't think about marriage or love before graduation. Master yourself and be the master of your life.

January 11

If love is a dream, I wouldn't feel so much pain when awake.

It was still blowing so hard when I went to the village market for some tea. The village was sound asleep while I was totally awake. I walked quietly on the muddy street and fell in love with this village. The sun had come out to smile at a sick me. I am ill because I have thought too much. I long for kisses, long to be loved and cared for. Without love, I would be like a girl without blood! I miss No. 4 who used to hug me so warmly when I was in trouble with Monitor. Sometimes sympathy and understanding are more useful than pills.

How I wish Clinton had gone further! If he kissed me first I wouldn't have been captured by Monitor. But, alas, silly Confucius principles bond Clinton so tightly. He has already given his nature up to traditions and bookish images. Monitor is a careless dandy. I knew it when he held my chin up in his hands and kissed me. His eyes were shining with greed which made me strangely sad. I had no time to cross-examine my heart before he prickled my infatuation. I was so ready and eager for love. I was a victim to the slightest temptation. Now he is tired of me. How cold am I when I think of the bleak future waiting for me! I need to be loved and I need to love. I am sure it is love that makes life worth living.

Alas, where is my love now? Sway in the wind!

January 12

I am better today. I search my heart and mind to find out that I am but a simple girl like the young romantic poet Xu zhimo. Mr. Xu wrote that popular poem *Farewell to Cambridge* and died in a plane crash. His poems are beautiful. He compared the waving willow in the wind to a bride in the setting sun. So full of love, just like himself.

My oldest uncle on my father's side came to chat. He talked about his children who also had experienced so many dramas of love. I have realized for the first time that romances could happen everywhere even in my village in the remote countryside.

January 13

I got up a little earlier this morning and read *the 21st century*. Most of the news is about government funds and charity for students in poverty. I am ashamed to realize that I am eligible to be one of those unlucky dogs. But I won't ask for help in this way. If a man is a successful, he must have his own belief and manage to get through every difficulty that is hindering his way up. Without economic condition love is a fish without water. So, love is beautiful but I cannot touch it now. I also listened to a record of a movie in *Crazy English* named *Waterloo Bridge*. I know that true love must be pure, very very pure. It's worth a life to be honest to.

After breakfast Mother and I went to see my grandparents. They still live in the old village half way on a small hill. It is a different world, a more backward and piteous one. To celebrate the coming Lantern Festival the farmers had set up a simple stage in the field and invited a troupe to perform some century old plays. I stood among the audience, crying. The players were so piteous. They tried their best to amuse the audience who were mostly toothless elders. The simple and backward troupe acted old plays for the aging people. They were both much neglected now. I stood there seeing the helpless struggle of survival of the old and was moved to tears by their rag dirty clothes and the hysterical appeal to the new changing world. I also went to the village temple nearby. There were two old women by the clay table where the incense was burnt. They were making paper flowers for the temple god. There were some lucky strings hanging over the table. Mothers usually come to kneel down before the sacred statue and ask for a string for their children. My mother was too busy with pigs and crops to do this, so I never had the chance to wear a bundle of lucky string. And that is probably why I have been so unlucky!

Grandma is 82 years old now. I think it is a pity to grow so old. She is not clear in her mind and seldom speaks. Sometimes she is forgotten even by her daughters. I sat there holding her soft clumsy hands. How I wanted to tell her that if she could insist on living for four more years I would earn lots of money to buy her all the delicious food and beautiful clothes. But I said nothing because her mind was not clear and nor is the future.

January 14

I was woken up quite early by the roosters far and near. I lay in bed, thinking of the details of my first love experience (if it can be called a love). There are still three and half years for me and Monitor to stay in the same classroom. If my heart is not given to another romance I wouldn't have the courage to give up Monitor and it is bad for both of us. So I have to find a refugee for my boiling imagination. I will turn back again to Clinton who used to love me so much and called me his rose. Clinton's campus is in the countryside and very far from mine. So, let him take away my wild imagination and leave me to study quietly. Well, on a second thought, I have lost interest in all the boys. Maybe the one who belongs to me has not appeared yet. I should save my feelings and love for him. I should keep silent and wait for that moment.

Then my dearest playmate Qin came. I have been expecting her since I came home on the first day. She is working with a very low pay in town and came back for the Lantern Festival. As the custom goes, her fiancé has asked her to celebrate the festival with his family which has made her mother angry. She is not in favor of the possible marriage with the boy who is short and not very rich. But Qin's father has used up all the money given to Qin by the boy's family as the dowry fee. Qin told me that two other boys in the workplace had fell in love with her and turned from good friends to rivals. She smiled while I scolded her. She said since boys can flirt with girls why can't girls do it too? I agreed with her. However she sighed at the end that maybe she would get hurt in this way so she needed a way out. That was why she didn't refuse an engagement with her short fiancé. It was difficult for me to say anything about the whole situation. I wanted to do something for her but I did not know how. I just looked at her and smiled and thought in my heart: she is my friend, a part of me. I came home and sat on the bench silently. I need nothing and nor do I think of anything.

Then evening came and my little niece Apricot begged me to take her out to show her red lantern.[4] I agreed and held her

---

4 The Lantern Festival falls on January 15, in lunar calendar. On this day people usually eat sweet dumplings and hang red lanterns. After this festival the Spring Festival ends officially.

hand and walked from the north of the village to the south. A few houses had hanged big red lanterns at the front gate and some villagers were still busy with lanterns. They climbed to the top of the ladder and tied red lanterns to the roof. But there weren't many children showing off like Apricot. She was disappointed. I tried to cheer her up and made her giggle so loud that the quiet air was stirred up. Oh, Lantern Festival, what is the meaning of it? The older I grow the more tasteless the traditional festivals seem to me. People are confusedly struggling in a "Market economy". Gradually, money has taken the place of trust and simple happiness in our hearts. Didn't Mother quarrel with my aunt and cut the relationship of the two families for money? Wasn't my dear eldest sister treated with contempt by her relatives because of her piteous situation? O, my dear China, where are you leading your lost lambs? When I was at my niece Apricot's age, there were so many children playing together. But now Apricot is alone. She clings to me who still has some childish fancies in heart. The girls at my age are all invited to spend the day with their fiancés. The village is left to the elderly and me. It is colder than usual.

January 15

After breakfast I had a walk on the roof of our house. Suddenly an idea struck me---the meaning of living is to find another part of you. It's a hard task which needs effort greater even than your life.

I went to the country fair at the end of the village in the afternoon with Apricot. I bought her a bag of instant noodles which she liked very much. However, on our way back we saw a lunatic who was laughing and searching the dustbin for food. He was so piteously happy that we stopped to watch him. I was sick at such a pathetic scene, so was Apricot. I encouraged her to give the instant noodles to him and she did it obediently.

We played fireworks in the evening and tried in vain to recollect my childhood pleasure. So we'd better enjoy ourselves in time otherwise age will take away the simple happiness before we know it.

Good night, all the loving people, sane or insane.

January 17

I will leave home for school early tomorrow morning. I begin to miss the days at home now. I've not been kind to my parents and felt very bad about it.

I still can't sleep alone so I asked Apricot to accompany me. I like her very much. I like her silk skin and innocent laughter. I kissed her on the face and she returned my kiss with her cherry-like lips and a giggle. She asked me where I came from. I told her I come from China and I am a Chinese. I asked her the same question but she told me she came from a foreign country! After all a child is a child. She suddenly got up and went to sleep with her grandma. It is so unexpected and strange. Maybe I shouldn't talk about death to her. I told her all lives would become a grain of dust in the end. Maybe she thought I was insane!

Chapter Three

Turning a New Leaf

January 19

Back in my classroom now. Life opens a new page for me. I am confident and eager to learn new things. The way back to school was full of anecdotes. Mother went to the village stop with me. We waited and waited but the bus just refused to come. I had plenty of time to review my dear dirty village and the rising sun. It crept out of the mountain top and jumped onto the street and covered the muddy and shabby country fair with so much warmth and splendor. It made me think of the day when my brother ran out of the clinic before the injection was over just to see me off to school. Our old house was burnt to ashes and my brother was trying to rebuild his confidence and a new house with borrowed money. He was so sick and tired that he caught a high fever. He was in a small clinic having injections while I was waiting for the bus to school. When he knew that I was leaving, he ran out to tell me that I was the hope of our family. I must study hard and have a position in this world. I remember the sun was pouring down its golden light as it was doing this time. There was so much hope and beauty and strength in its generous splendor. I was moved to tears. Yes, dear brother, I will work hard for your trust and honor.

When my eyes caught Zhengzhou University's broad iron gate something profound and heroic choked me. I murmured to myself: I am home now. I am back to my world now, a world of knowledge, truth and perseverance.

My roommates yelled happily when I walked into the dorm. The feud of the two sides was totally forgotten during the winter vacation. I am at "my home" at last!

January 23

My cheeks are very hot now. I am a little excited this evening because I just made an announcement to the class in English. I was too nervous to speak slowly and clearly. After that I read *Emma* aloud until I was too tired to open my mouth. If English is a pie I would like to wolf it down within one second but it is a huge mountain. I have to huff and puff, yet I am still at the foot of the mountain.

January 26

I listened to the radio last night and wanted to cry when I heard a poem by Xi Murong. She said when people fall in love they must love each other tenderly. If they have to part they should also say goodbye gently. I feel empty and upset. I am afraid I have to say goodbye to Monitor and wish it will be a gentle one.

January 27

My world fell apart last night when Monitor stayed the whole night out with No. 4. He abandoned me and took away my dear friend! How hurt my heart was and still is! I can't comprehend it. I hate him! I hate him! He is a serpent. I must keep cool. I want someone to hug me tightly. The world is so cold and dark. Be yourself, Pearl, don't cry. Smile to him as if you don't care a damn of what he is doing. He has never loved you but your lips! My heart is crying but no tears come out. My eyes have already gone dry last term.

The setting sun, the slow melody, worries, sorrows, hopes......all are so upset and beautiful.

February 2

Today is Monitor's birthday. I spent 20 Yuan to buy him a bunch of flowers. I was sad at my pretentious generosity. Why did I do this since he had been so unfaithful to me? Why did I say happy birthday to him when I wanted so much to punch his playboy face? Am I insane?

February 7

The wound Monitor cut in my heart begins to swell after the first few days of self-licking. The world is upside down before my eyes and I don't have any strength to make it right. I am so weak, stupid and helpless. I am dying for pure love but when I called Clinton he didn't answer me. Well, sometimes we have to stand on our own feet though my feet are so shaky now. I love myself so I must be myself!

February 8

I am beautiful today--- eyes big and shining; skirt new and smart; hair clean and fluffy. Well, alas, there is no one to appreciate me.

February 16

When I was in the dorm, a girl came to sell a governess job. I followed her on my bike to that family which she had introduced. It was blowing dusts and fallen leaves were dancing wildly in the wind. I narrowed my eyes to see the way. It was so far away I wanted to give up before I reached the destination. However, I rode on until we stopped in front of a dingy and small apartment. The woman invited us to her home and explained that she and her husband were both laid off. They put all their hope on the daughter who, with thick glasses on, was sitting furiously at the dark corner of the tiny room. It was obvious that they can't offer a good pay. Six Yuan one hour! Sorry, I couldn't accept it. It was not worthy of the time and energy though I pitied the girl very much. On the way back I lost my way and got wrong directions from kindhearted devils. I almost collapsed at the sight of Zhengzhou University after 5 hours of riding in the dusts.

February 18

A terrible and exciting day.

I was so eager for its coming, but when it came I was too

nervous to give my best performance. Anyhow, I hosted the English Speaking Contest for the first time. Maybe I made a fool of myself but thank God I made it.

March 31

It is raining now, in my heart as well as outside the window. I was so happy in the fresh morning, riding a bike and speaking English to myself. But suddenly tears fell down. I was so lonely without love and friendship. My story was in a mess and my world was unbalanced. A girl from another dorm came to comfort me. She said human beings should have dignity and pride. It was silly of me to cling to a dead romance while the male actor had run happily away.

April 2

Don't be so serious with life, Pearl. There are no clear-cut answers to all the puzzles. Just enjoy yourself, for the purpose of life is to be happy. This is the end of the play. People won't say I am right because my lover runs away with my friend or he will be punished for his hypocrisy. There is no justice in this complicated world and some people enjoy seeing wrongs and revenge. I must say goodbye to them and move on. Don't be a stubborn mule anymore. Change myself and concentrate on my English study. This week I will finish reading the Bible and make a plan for the next step.

April 26

I am like a wild animal. I demand to be free and to do whatever I want to do. And I have done lots of silly things in this train of thought. Now it's time for me to wake up. Someone has introduced me a new governess job. My student is a handsome and young salesman Mr. Li.

At the first sight of me he said I was too pure and simple to do this kind of job. What? I've been a governess before. He cast down his long and black eye lashes and said I was his savior. He would turn a new leaf from that day. Would you please call me Turning? Of course, I said. So this was how I knew Mr. Turning. So funny and strange! And, he is the most handsome man I have ever seen. He reminds me so much of my little prince---an adult version.

May 21

I talked with my new friend Rebecca tonight and found myself lacking of many virtues--- not pious enough to knowledge, too close to boys and too loose with money.

May 24

What a disaster! I told Mr. Turning that I liked him and he said "concentrate on your study! Don't think too much!" without hesitation. I pricked the beautiful ball of fancies with needles, and so early! I felt dead on the spot and took the trolley back to school nonchalantly. My senses were all numbed. I left my feet on the narrow passage to be stepped on by high heels and did not pretest at all when a fat mother pushed her child on my seat. I was dead, but came back to life when I entered the classroom and opened my English book.

June 11

Sometimes I am so dissatisfactory with myself that I hate to see my face in the mirror, hate to hear my own voice and hate to feed myself with chopsticks. It is an awkward period. I am not mature enough for my wild imagination and demand a quick leap-forward of my mind.

July 6

Summer vacation will start soon. Many students want to stay for a miracle---a temporary job and big money for next year's tuition. I am one of them. I've enrolled my name in dozens of agencies for a governess job. So far no one has called me.

It's very hard for my friends and me to find a job in this poor and crowded city. We live a simple and humble life of eating cheap food, walking long walks and waiting without any hope. There is no beacon light in my life.

I went to the city square this evening and lost myself in missing Mr. Turning. I quitted my part-time job as his governess after that thoughtless confession. He asked his friend to tell me that he had left Zhengzhou for a business trip and would come back to see me as soon as possible. Well, really? I doubt it. Anyhow it won't be wrong to have a splendid dream. So I count the days but this Mr. Turning never turns up.

Sometimes I am sure that we should do what we like and let others know if we like them, as what I did to Turning. But sometimes I am not so sure. To be honest is not the best policy.

Chapter Four

Swirling a Black Skirt

July 7

Summer vacation has finally come. Having nothing to do, I turned on the radio. Qi Qin's melancholy voice flew out: *with what shall I love you? I don't know.* I have nothing except a naive belief in love and shallow taste in beauty. How I miss Turning---his down casting eyes and round healthy body! How I miss his voice but the phone is always silent.

Yingzi (a dear old friend from high school) and I went shop after shop to look for an assistant job for her. But no one wanted us. At last we went to an agent for help. There were three men eating water melon when we entered the small and suspicious office. They learned our situation and agreed to help if Yingzi gave them 70 Yuan service fee on the spot. We didn't expect that and stood there biting our lips. They saw we were students and began to make funs of us. I was set on fire and quarreled with them till each of my limbs trembled. They were so taken aback by this young bull that they gave up their water melon and started to comfort us by talking about their hometown in the north-east of China. I made peace with them on knowing that they came from the same place as Turning. Everything concerning him is tolerable. From this confront I know I want time and knowledge. Without time I can't grow up. Without knowledge I am not confident or attractive. I will try hard to get Turning. But where is he now? Is he missing me?

July 8

So many college students are fighting for scant summer jobs. I can't see any hope of making money this vocation, nor can Ben. We had a walk around the playground and the more we walked the more piteous we became.

When I walked back to the dorm the phone rang. It was my sister. She said all the families miss me, "Come back if you can't find a job in Zhengzhou". I laughed and told her I was quite well and would find a job soon. She said Dad and Mum miss me. They checked the calendar every day and counted the days of my coming back. No, I won't go home until I earn some money to buy them a few gifts at least. In this way I have forced myself to stay. How I miss my parents! The more I miss them, the more I want to postpone my going back. Let my love for Dad and Mum become strength that will help me squeeze into this jobless city.

July 10

An old classmate at senior high school named Gang will come to see me. He is a college student in Beijing. He used to sit in front of me. My only memory about him is that he once dropped a candy over his shoulder to my desk and said nothing about it. He has written me several letters to say he has had a crush for me since long ago. I am flattered at this sweet revelation for he was quite a hot potato at that time. However, I don't want to be involved in love affairs right now and I have told him so. Poor boy, he must be hurt.

This afternoon I found a job and will start working tomorrow. Yingzi hasn't found one and she has to go home. I listened to *Ghost* and missed Turning. We are living in two worlds and he won't be able to come back to me. Only silence can make me a mature woman.

July 16

I went to a park near the campus last night with a boy named Harvey. He was introduced to me by a classmate. I was so determined to be happy that I put on the long black skirt and swirled before him till he kissed me. Wow, I am a wicked girl sometimes. We spent the whole night among the bushes in the park, talking and hugging. I pretended to be so docile yet my heart was laughing secretly at his red face and clumsy kiss. Suddenly it began to rain in the early morning. We walked in half- knee deep water to school. He was totally changed by the night or the rain, but I was not. He bought me a towel and dried my face and hair silently and ran away.

July 17

Harvey asked me to have a walk with him around the city square. I captured him last night with my long black skirt. Tonight he was mine, a lovely and honest cat! I was so happy! Good night all my friends!

July 18

I dreamed of Harvey all the night. He has opened a new world for me, so pure and so true. My girlish dream for Clinton is over. He is positioned as a big brother now. Turning has also been put up on the shelf for keeping. Harvey is the first boy who says "I love you" to me.

July 19

Gang finally came to Zhengzhou and asked me to hang around with him in the afternoon and bought me a pair of new sandals. He was a handsome and smart boy, but, alas, too late for me. I was still trying to come out of Monitor's bad shadow when he wrote me the first love letter. Now Harvey, my poor prince, had kissed on my lips so that I can't help but say no when Gang came in person to ask me again and again would I be his girlfriend. He sighed and left.

July 20

How time flies when I am surrounded by handsome boys! I've wasted a lot of my precious youth in dating, missing and worrying. This vacation is fresh and strange. I can't resist the temptation of enjoying life. I want to give others happiness and in the meantime make myself feel good. My roommates have scolded me. They thought I was too naive and careless. Well, everything has two sides. I've known so many people. I give them love and they return me with kindness and care. What's wrong with this? But somehow I feel like decaying and long for my quiet and lonely days.

July 21

I called Harvey just now. There is a kind of gentle and touching feeling between us.

Gang came again tonight. I came downstairs with a sister's smile on my face. The best relationship for us is to be sister and brother. It's not in my nature to give boys a cold shoulder if I can't return their love. I give them something similar. A person should be grateful. And, Gang is so gentle and patient with me.

There is a world in my heart. No one can reach it. Sometimes even I can't see it clearly but I have felt it this afternoon.

July 23

I spent the whole night with Harvey yesterday. We walked and walked till the stars came out and then the sun rose up. His kiss was strong and tender. I am sure he likes me. Then in the afternoon I took Trolley 101 to see Turning. He was back from the business trip and invited me to dinner. His assistant received me at the station. We waited for a long time before Turning appeared, still so handsome and energetic. I tried to keep a calm and smiling face though my heart was beating so fast and so sadly. I observed him ardently across the dinner table. I can't help it. Don't people turn to the shining sun naturally? His neat T shirt, big and black eyes, clean and white hands, and his proud but funny air....I was not looking at a man but at a piece of artwork that I had never seen in my life. He tried to avoid my fervent eyes but he couldn't. He stopped his busy chopsticks and asked me, "Why are you looking at me?""Because I like you," I answered honestly. Other boys at the table were amused. Turning turned red but tried to cover his shaky heart by throwing me an empty bottle while saying jokingly, "Take this, a gift to you". I wondered what he meant by this but continued my meal like a cold and majestic queen. I drank him with my eyes to the full and excused myself while they were still having their beer. Turning came out and stopped a taxi for me. For a moment he was tender and loving. He gave the driver 10 Yuan and insisted him to take me to the north gate of Zhengzhou University. So I left my sun with unspeakably sadness. It was crystal clear that he did not like me at all. I felt so bankrupt and called Harvey for some comfort. Harvey is my equal. I am not tense or too excited when we are together.

Yangzi (my adult student) came to study English with me. While she was half asleep, I translated her three love letters from the US. It was a difficult task. It was the first time I saw live English from a true American and the expressions he used were so different from what I learned in textbooks. Yangzi knew nothing about my uneasiness but entrusted her love story to an English major. I am ill with the pressure. I am still a beginner in English after 10 years study. I can't speak it fluently nor can I write it beautifully. How can I improve myself? How? How? I force my spinning head to think but couldn't find an answer.

Today that bad Monitor came back from the vacation, bringing back all my sadness and hatred. He is a false one. I know it clearly but my roommates like him and talk happily about him to my face. It is cruel. But sometimes girls are really cruel animals. They can't help it. It is in their nature to enjoy other's torture and pain. Why do I have to live with these heartless girls? It's a shame that I have to live with them in the same tiny room and use the same toilet. How I want to escape to a place full of understanding, kindness and sunshine! But I can't escape. The only way for me is to live miserably and let others live heartlessly.

July 23

Yesterday morning the war broke out in the dorm. My fabulous roommates dared to talk evil of me in Rui's face! Rui was angry and argued with them. They believed I was a wanton girl who went out with boys and did bad things! They said I deserved Monitor's coldness for he was such an honest fellow. Shit! Pure shit! How can I bear such a hideous verdict! I burst into tears and yelled, hysterically, "Where are your hearts? Do you have any feelings? Do you know what sympathy means? How can you be so cruel! Shame on you all!" No.3 became silent and No.6 began to cry. Why should she cry? I didn't know. I let my boiling stream out and left the dorm. Suddenly I felt so empty. I was so alone in this world.

August 6

I am lazy and tired. Friends are like wind. They come and go. Feelings and friendship do not mean much in this "market economy". How much is your love for me? How much does your "miss" mean to me? Mmm, not very much. Something has changed so drastically in China. Families begin to separate and go their own ways. People are saying farewell to the cordial and warm past to make their great expectations in the heartless future.

August 9

I went to the east gate of the campus to sell myself as a governess. Parents came and looked into the thirsting and even begging eyes of the student teachers as if we were slaves who just came on board from Africa. A woman came forward to me and another girl. She asked me what I could teach. "English," I said. "How much an hour?" she asked me while polishing her scarlet nails. "Ten Yuan," I answered calmly. "I will do for you six Yuan an hour!" the girl near me thrust in. I turned to see a sharp chin and a pair of thin and dry lips. She looked so desperate to have a job. I didn't hate her at all but pitied her. The nail polisher glanced at her scornfully and turned to me again. "What about eight Yuan?" she asked me again. "No," I said, wishing her to take the girl with dry lips which she did. While the woman and the girl student were negotiating, another woman came up to me. She looked like a typical kind mother who gave her flesh and blood to her children. She smiled at me and asked me whether I would go to live with her family so that I could help her son with his English for a month. I hesitated. She waved to a man near a car. He came up with her ID card which she asked me to check. I refused to see the card but I believed her. I can feel a person instantly. She was a kind lady. Yes, I would go with her. She was so happy and promised to wait for me at the gate while I ran back to the dorm to pack. Her house was in the suburb of the city. I put some clothes and books into my humble bag and entered their car. She familiarized me with her son's situation during the hour's drive. He was under great pressure of the college entrance exam and not very well. She hinted to me not to be hard on her sensitive boy. Let him learn easily and happily. Then I was in their well-decorated house. A new challenge began.

August 9

The first day with my new student Fei. He is a gentle boy and eager to learn. In helping Fei with English grammar and basic words I spent another day in a stranger's home. In the afternoon, Fei's friend came to see him so we finished quickly and I went out to have a walk. In fact I was hungry. I don't know how to "make myself at home" at a new place. I tried to be modest and said "I am full" when I was still half hungry. I walked in the lonely street and bought three pancakes. I ate and wandered like a tramp. How many times have I walked like this?

Unexpectedly sad.

August 11

I dreamed of Turning last night. He murdered a man and

went abroad to hide. Just like Scarlet in *Gone with the Wind* I said to myself, "I can get him. I must get him. I will never be happy until I find him." But I am so poor and simple now. Even if I have found him I can't make him appreciate me. So I must improve myself. I don't want to hurt Harvey but we are not of the same kind". What a strange dream! My God, give me wisdom and strength.

I was struck by the horror of death again in my nap. I wanted so much to be with Turning at that moment, otherwise life seemed so meaningless. How I wish he could have experienced what I was experiencing then, so that he can understand my helpless attachment to him! Alas, even if he could accept me, I can't give myself up like this. I looked in the mirror and found a piteous and ugly face. What is the use of beautiful feelings when men only value pretty faces!

I miss the freedom of my own home and the natural pleasure with my little nieces and nephews. Fei and his parents are kind to me but I just can't relax under other people's roof. I will study. Knowledge is a bridge to Turning , to England and to many many wonderful places.

August 12

Another day is passing quickly when I wake up from my dream. I hope my student can make great progress with English. His parents wish him to be a dragon in the future and he is so anxious to please his dear Mum who runs to him at his faintest sigh. This afternoon I bought a smart note book for him and urged him to keep English journals in it. I wanted to buy myself something too but I didn't. My pocket was always empty recently.

It is one o'clock in the early morning. I am wet with sweat. I get up, turn on the neon light of my room and drink a glass of cold water. I walk to the window and see the dark field with my mind's eye. The cry of night birds is mysterious and scary. The noise of summer insects reminds me of my hometown. How I miss my waves and waves of golden wheat, my black cow and my dear little friends! How time has changed every one of us! I sit on the cement floor and weep.

August 14

This morning I urged Fei to read aloud on the grassland near his house. He was such a delicate child. I believed fresh air would do him good. Unfortunately, it began to rain. We had to run back after half an hour's reading. Even the half hour's exposure to open air did us a lot of good. We were both starving before lunch was ready and I couldn't afford to be modest any longer. I ate to my heart's content and to Fei's mother's surprise. After lunch I watched TV for a short time. A program of college life was on. It was really just a show. All the college students were so docile, idealistic and rich! What a farce! The director of this movie should come to our campus to see the real college students who work under the heavy burden of loan and competition and struggle vainly in a love not so puppy as in the movie but more fierce and more complicated than adult's love . I gave up the movie and walked to the window. Some hands were stretching out from the opposite building. Some peasant workers were decorating the newly-finished building. They were in rags and with dirt on their hands, yet it seemed to me that they were more powerful and noble than the puppet students in the play.

August 15

Fei's mother said that Fei was too ill to study and she planned to take him for a trip. She gave me 200yuan for my work and I took a bus back to school. It happened that Rui was going home tomorrow. Rui was teaching math. The father of her student molested her when his wife was not there. She thought it was too risky to stay with that family. So she quit and we are going home together.

August 16

I am home now, very tired. How I want to get engaged to a rich man so that I don't need to worry about tuition anymore! Poverty is the fact, life is meaningless and money is God. I need money to go on with my study and to feel good about being alive. What can I do? Get engaged to a rich man! I am so bad to think of such a thing when Harvey is so kind to me. But, alas, where can my poor father find 5,000 Yuan for the new school year?

Now I'm listening to the broadcast on the flood near Yangzi River area. It is an unprecedented disaster. Many ripen crops have been swept away. Millions of people have to migrate to another place. Compared with their difficulty, mine seems not so formidable after all. Our yard is full of flowers. They look so beautiful in the rain. I sit beside them with an umbrella over my head and think of Harvey.

August 18

Father and mother have put up the mosquito net for me. I lie on my wooden bed and feel really at home now.

Yesterday was a busy day. I went to see my brother and sister-in-law. They were hiding in the fields to produce a male heir for the Liu family. They have been hiding here and there for three years and have produced another girl. My sister-in-law has refused to go home without producing a boy. She thinks it a shame for a family without a male heir. So they hide in a deserted house among high grassland. Without my brother's instruction I wouldn't believe there were human beings in that shabby clay house. Poor woman, will you produce a dragon here? My brother's love and protection for me are absolute but he is as poor as my father. I can't open my mouth and ask for money from him. My mother has pressed him hard enough for money. Father put down his dignity to borrow money from those few rich relatives and friends. It was a torture for him. The family is already under a heavy debt for the new house. Oh, I am a murderer. I have to murder so many people's happiness to continue my study. My mother is like a fierce hen. She tries to collect enough food for her poor little chicken and quarrels with those who refuse to help her. Father is so tired. He told me he was ill for the first time in my life. What shall I do?

August 20

The gap between the rich and the poor is so huge that some desperate young men decide to revenge. It's rumored that more than 20 rich families have been murdered within three months. The rich families in my village are so scared that they throng into hotels and appeal for collective protection. The head of the village demands that each family should offer a male adult to patrol the street by turns at night. Tonight is my father's turn. Mother went to see my grandparents in the morning. I will be left alone. I am too timid to endure the darkness alone so I ask a neighbor girl come to share my bed. At 7 pm he took a drum and went out. My neighbor came to be my company but she fell asleep once her head was on the pillow. I lay there, fear- stricken. Suddenly I hear someone scratching my door! I opened my eyes wide and held my breath. He was still there, trying his keys in the keyhole! No, I can't bear it anymore! "Who's there?" The scratching on the door stopped but no one answered. I turned on the light and went to the door. Taking a deep breath I opened the door. Thank God, no sticks came down my head. A little mouse slipped away. Pooh, it was you, you little devil! I left the door open and went to bed again.

August 21

It's raining now. The flowers and fruits in our yard are standing in the rain. I don't know whether they are cold or not. My second sister came to give me 500 Yuan. It is the money her mother-in-law gave her to see the doctor. The money weighs so heavy on my hand and in my heart.

August 23

I am silent again, as silent as a dead volcano. No matter what my parents say I refuse to comment. Do I have the right to comment on anything when I am the burden of the family? No. I don't even have the mood to be happy or to laugh. Father felt sorry for me. He made a mark on the calendar of my leaving day and sighed, "My poor girl, we haven't made you any delicious food yet". Thus he went to the market to buy oil so that mother could fry some eggs for me. I closed the door to my room and cried silently under the quilt.

My two best playmates Qin and Ping are engaged and will marry into other villages soon. Most girls at my age are married. I am left behind. I still go to sit on the stone bench at the end of the lane, still roam about the wild fields and deep valley and still stick new pictures on the wall when the Spring Festival comes. However, am I still the same person? How time flies! I am sure when I come home again for the vacation, Qin and Ping will be mothers. It is the rule of China----if you don't have much to do, go producing babies. Babies are hopes. Disappointed people are more inclined to produce babies. Babies bring hope for a meaningless life. Shall I get engaged to someone rich? I was nicknamed romantic fairy at senior high school. Now the fairy has come down to earth. I do not connect marriage with love but with money. What a shame!

August 24

Qin called on me after breakfast. I was so happy to see her. My coming home won't be perfect without seeing her at least once. She will get married to that short man this winter and she is not happy at all. She said gloomily that life was meaningless. I told her that I wanted to be engaged to a rich man so that he could support me to continue my education. She objected strongly and encouraged me to study with a pure heart. We talked little. I was too worried about my tuition while she was not interested in anything. I couldn't make myself understood or tell her the meaning of life. We are friends, very old friends. We do not need to talk much but we can feel each other's sorrows by instinct.

It's still raining. A peony blooms secretly in the darkness. I bend down and kiss it.

August 26

"I want to be a bride, a happy bride. Then my dream will have a direction. I can fly happily and I will have a home." This *Happy Bride* song speaks to my heart.

This morning I went to the field to see whether our corn was ready for harvesting. On the way back home I found some purple flowers on the muddy ground and picked them up. Watching carefully I couldn't help but admire the perfect design on the petals. I picked some grass to go with the purple flowers and went home with beauty. Then a little girl saw me and begged me to give her a flower. I was happy to have a good home for the abandoned flowers and gave them all to her. How easily I made the girl happy!

To avoid washing dishes I finished my lunch quickly and went out to relax. At the gate I found a branch of golden chrysanthemums bent over the short wall. Some had already withered, some were still alive. I picked four and went out. I felt so free, natural and comfortable with these flowers in hand. Coming out of the small lane I saw a tear- stricken face. A cute little girl was crying because she was late for school. I asked her, "Do you want these flowers?" She stopped crying, stretched out her little hand and took the flowers without hesitation. I smiled. The flowers took a lot of her attention. She was still sobbing but not so earnest now. Ah, what a touching picture! Isn't the teacher lucky to see a cute little girl with four golden flowers standing at her door? Innocent children and beautiful flowers become the day! When I walked by the withered branch I took another three chrysanthemums, one red, one golden and one green. They were for myself. I put them in a vase and put the vase on my window sill.

I tried to have a nap but can't fall asleep no matter how hard I tried. So I got up and went out to the yard. There I found my mother was cutting Qin's mother's hair for her. She had a towel around her neck and a slice of broken mirror in her hand. The Family Planning Committee of the village smashed my brother's wardrobe and furniture when they couldn't find him. Mother collected some pieces of the broken mirror. I looked at myself in one of the bigger pieces. Ah, so funny, I could see only one ear! Qin's mother was like a little girl. She looked herself in the mirror and complained it was too small for her big face and giggled happily with mother. For a moment they forgot about husbands and children. They were teenagers again who had only themselves to worry and to treasure. I didn't want to interrupt them so I went back to my room and to the thinking of Turning and Harvey. Turning is a dream and Harvey is a reality. Dreams are splendid but unstable which make me sometimes happy sometimes sad but mostly mad. Reality is warm and reliable which draws me back to earth. When feelings marry reality, life is produced. While feelings and dreams give birth to love. I need a happy life as well as a romantic love. Greedy? Not sure. I am so contradictory. I want with all my heart to be a lady while my nature is so careless and wild. Who can love me when my skin is not smooth or my face delicate? Why am I not a flower dancing in the wind?

It's so quiet. I can hear raindrops patting pumpkin leaves and one or two songs from autumn insects. It's evening now, time to weave dreams and to be drunk. It's time for the soul to return to the body and it is time for truth.

August 26

Thank God it was still raining when I decided to sell some umbrellas in the early morning. It was my third time to sell things in the country fair. I sold leek when I was in primary school and earned 1.7 Yuan, and then I sold grapes when in high school but earned nothing. It was like killing me to sit in the dirty and poor market and wait hopelessly for buyers. This morning I went to kill myself for the third time and did not sell any umbrella. I can never be a successful merchant. I am too silly and too proud for such a challenging profession. We are so poor. My tuition is like the sword hanging over my parents' head. If there is really no other way to go I want to be engaged to my "little prince" who is not little anymore but still a prince. My fantasies were attached to his shining black eyes and round big head. His family is well-to-do. But, but, will I spend my life in the countryside? No, compared to the future and long-term happiness, money is not that important after all. I was very eager to see him when I was back to the village. Yet now, when I am listening to English songs I think of my college life, my friends, and my study. I am so sad inside. I am so so confused. God, what is love? Now I am still young but one day I will be old like the withered flowers on the wet bough. By the way, are my flowers lonely in the cold darkness? I am lost in thought yet I am thinking nothing. Dream is too far and reality is too troublesome. Sometimes we just don't have anything to do and nothing needs us to do. Like this morning, I sat beside my umbrellas. I just sat there, not particularly waiting for any buyers.

August 27

It's 3 o'clock in the morning. I really don't want to waste my eyes, but no matter how hard I try I just can't fall asleep. My memory of the past gets more and more clear with the darkness of the night. So I am here in a chair now in the open air. I have seldom had a full sleep since I came back home and tomorrow I will be leaving.

Several hours ago I stood in front of the small temple at the end of the village with Ping's sister. She sang many of my favorite songs for me in the rain. Oh, my dear friends on this piteous and dry land, how many dreams you have, yet how many have become bubbles!

The flowers in my cup are still alive and fresh but I am leaving. The diligent roosters of the countryside are showing off their piercing voices. It is still very dark, very dark.

Chapter Five

Love Made Cannot be Unmade

August 28

Back to Room 202. I was the first one here. I ran to the telephone and called Turning. I planned to borrow 500 Yuan from him for Ben who was worried to death about the tuition. Yet no one answered. Who else can I turn to? Yangzi? Maybe. I called her but she was not there either. Then I called Harvey, Gosh, he hadn't come back to school yet. I called Ben, he was out. In the end I had to sit on my bed quietly. Then I went to the classroom. Ben was there. He was so happy to see me that tears stung my eyes at his honest and eager face. I must help him with the tuition. I called Yangzi again and found her. She promised to give me 800 Yuan as my pay for the translation of love letters.

August30

Clinton came here this afternoon to tell me that he was trying to borrow some money for the tuition so he couldn't pay me back the 50 Yuan I gave him last time. Of course I showed my understanding and sympathy. I was so sad that I couldn't help him. He went melancholy back to his school, and I stood here thinking helplessly about all my poor friends. How I wish I were a millionaire so that I can spread big notes of RMB among my dear friends and we shall all laugh and laugh heartedly.

August 31

The new semester started with boundless worries about money and a stronger desire for knowledge. Yangzi paid me 500yuan for my work and asked me to translate another four love letters from the US. She behaved like a proud princess this evening and was very critical of my English. I was so anxious to do a good job for her, not for her money but more for my pride. Harvey had to apply for a loan for the tuition. I wish I could be of some help to him. I called several former clients to see whether they still need governess. I am so stressed. Money, love letters, my English, my dear God, and, alas, my spinning head!

September 2

I am ill. I am tired and nonchalant the whole day. I drag my heavy legs from the classroom to the dorm room and to the dining hall and finally to the bank of the golden river which runs through the campus. I sit there thinking about my future. No, I can't see my future yet. I can't even see a friendly face among more than 8,000 students. I have no real friends here. Only Yangzi can give me a little girlish pleasure sometimes, but she is a dandy lady and changes her mood within ten minutes. As to the love letters, sorry,

I don't have any feelings for empty love talk now. I don't know whether I should be serious about life or take it easy.

September 3

Life is meaningless. I am not interested in anything now. My dream is vague and my knowledge limited. What shall I be? May God help me. Then the piteous pictures of the countryside children would come to scold me. How can I be so selfish? I am not living for myself nor should I be. I sobbed for a whole hour in the meeting room when a high school teacher invited me to give a lecture to the students. I entered the room and alas, what did I see? I saw honest faces, shabby clothes, humble eyes; I saw a group of pure lambs who mostly would not have a fair future; I saw dozens of Patricias sitting around me, sobbing. I was overwhelmed with something too strong for my heart to bear and too mysterious for my mind to comprehend. I sat among them but couldn't utter a word. Words were meaningless when the dreaded past came to present itself again. Now I have a chance to go to college. How dare I lose my dreams and forget people's great expectations for me? God, let me never forget that there is always a flower that is fragrant, always a drop of blood that is warm, always an affection that is true.

I have run out of money now. I wrote a letter just now asking Pretty for some help.

September 5

Harvey is with me now in my classroom. I have shown him

a poem---making friends. I hope one day when we have to say goodbye he will forgive me because of this hint I have given him tonight. He is such a simple boy and not ashamed of wasting time at all. I just can't bear seeing people doing nothing. So while I am reading I suggest that he write me a letter. A letter? Why? Why do I need to write a letter when you are here with me? He said contemptuously. Silly boy, use your imagination. Suppose I am in the US or other country now. Write me a letter to say how much you miss me! I am so annoyed at his mechanical mind. No, he prefers to bury his head in his arms and pretend to sleep than write me a love letter. What a log is this Harvey! Gosh, he is snorting now.

September 6

Last night I went to the park near the campus with Harvey. He kissed me fervently though I responded coldly. I had lost interest in kissing and told him so. After kissing and caressing I sat quietly gazing at the moon. I was sad. I didn't know what love was nor did I know whether I love Harvey or am just hurting him. I asked him how he felt when he kissed me. Was he happy? He dropped his head and murmured yes. I told him my mind and emphasized friendship between us. I didn't want to be a girl whose soul was far away from her body. He said nothing and went silently to his dorm. I was uneasy and called him this morning. He was so depressed that I hated myself for exposing the so called truth last night. Truth be hanged!

Then I wandered to the city square in the hot sun.

Immediately I saw the flower pots. The green Giant with wide leaves was believed to bring money for its owner. I was trying to save money to buy it for Turning when he disappeared. Now the Giant was still there but Turning was gone, leaving me wandering alone under the scorching sun. I couldn't remember how many times I had walked like this, without a destination or a purpose. Well I was quite at home with this deep loneliness now and walked quietly on a deserted square.

Then I wandered into a book shop where I found *Jane Eyre* by Charlotte Bronte. I once bought this book for Turning and underlined the most touching paragraphs, hoping he would love me as Mr. Rochester loved Jane when he heard her uttering these words. However, Turning was not Rochester though I compared myself to Jane.

Picking up a handful of sands and it will slip through your fingers. But love is deep in my heart and never slips away.

September 8

Yangzi came with two letters from Donald, an American from Alaska. He surfaced again after a month's disappearance. I translated his longing to her and her eyes began to shine instantly. The sad girl one hour ago was transfigured to a happy princess. I have to say love is like the sea and the two hearts are carried by waves, sometimes to the summit, sometimes to the deepest bottom of sorrow and doubt. The love across cultures is even harder. I wish everything would go well with Yangzi.

It has been so hot these days----time for me to express

myself. Yes, the summer always makes me excited. I would come to the empty and steaming classroom when others are having a nap. I sit and think and cry and write my love story with the title "*Sands in hands*". I seal it and post it to a university publisher who is collecting this kind of stories from college students.

September 13

Today is my birthday. No.3 stretched herself and murmured "Happy birthday No.2!" Then the other 6 lazy cats all woke up to wish me a happy birthday. I felt so good and privileged in this fresh and friendly morning. When I was combing, I noticed a card. It was from Six. Ah, why should life be so wonderful! Love alone can wake love. This morning is the brightest day since I came to Zhengzhou University. I've tasted the sweetness of being loved. At lunch time my name was heard in the broadcast. Ah, dear No. 6 and No.8 ordered a song for me! How wonderful to have Céline Dion sing for me! My love will go on.

It is the first time in my life to be so obviously loved by my friends. Harvey didn't buy me a birthday present and my roommates were not satisfied with him. May God bless my friends! I would live with hope and laughter and LOVE.

September 16

Our foreign teacher Patrick introduced an American boy Ryan to Rebecca and me. We paid him a third visit today but still did not see him. I was so disappointed at his carelessness that I even wanted to give up. But Rebecca wouldn't give up. She was determined to see this American boy who broke his promise again and again.

September 17

What kind of boy is this Ryan? We paid him the fifth visit this afternoon and he was still not in. Shall we call him again? Why do we have to be so active in making friends with foreign students? It is not my nature to be so aggressive. For English study? More than that. We are so eager to know the outside world and the western culture. Curiosity alone has enough strength to draw us to fair hair, blue eyes and childish walking style.

September 21

It's evening now. I just had a long walk with Rebecca. I always feel relaxed and happy with her. She is honest and ambitious. She encourages me to further my study abroad which is ridiculed by other students. How I want to enter another world--a world of sages who can appreciate beauty, truth and creativity!

September 22

This evening is terrifying. Rebecca and I would push ourselves to the gallows by visiting Amy—the strict American teacher.

What shall we say? Will she like us? I hesitated to call her yesterday. Whenever I picked up the phone, I felt sick at heart. I dread to offend people from different cultures and also dread to be hurt by others.

September 23

We visited Patrick and Amy last night. It was my first volunteer encounter with people from other countries and it was not so terrifying at all. Amy said Ryan was very homesick. So I forgave him at once and came to the dorm to call him. He received the phone and became very friendly when I shared his homesickness with him. We made an appointment at half past six tomorrow afternoon. Putting down the phone I was happy and nervous. I didn't know how to communicate with foreigners. What shall I do, Ryan? I hope you were a Chinese or I was an American so that we can understand each other without any guessing and doubting. But, East is East, and West is West. We can do nothing about it but face each other with lots of good wishes and nervousness.

September 24

This morning after the extensive reading class that bad monitor came to tell me that he wanted to be my desk mate when we take the Band 4 exam later. I was a fool to agree. I don't want to cheat at exams. No, I mustn't let him come near to me. He is a serpent.

September 26

Last night Ryan, Rebecca and I had dinner together. We used our pocket money to treat Ryan in a good restaurant. It was a great success.

September 27

Last night Harvey asked me to visit one of his friends with him. We arrived at a tiny and simple room in the late afternoon. His friend Hua was living together with his girlfriend. I was embarrassed to know that unmarried people can live together. But the girl was calm. She poured hot water for us like a common house wife. Then she went out to wash his clothes when we three were chatting and laughing. I felt sorry for her and hinted several times that we should leave. But Harvey was strangely excited and refused to leave. We talked and talked, and the poor girl was making a noise to let us go. At last I stood up and dragged Harvey out of the tiny room. It was totally dark outside and very cold. We wandered on the empty street, ready to take adventures. I was a little bit energetic in the chilly air but Harvey was nervous. He took out a cigarette and I lit it for him. Wow, we were like a really bad man and his bad wife. We searched the street but could not find a video room where love birds usually build their nests. At last we went far into the wild field and sat under the roof of a deserted house. Darkness and smoke were provoking and exciting. Harvey kissed me affectionately on my lips, my face and my neck. His small eyes were filled with glistering happiness and tears. He whispered "let's make love!" I covered my face while he undressed me. It was so strange and silly to let a boy see my body. I trembled with coldness and fear. Within a second he finished it and I was fully dressed again. I sat there, tired and empty and refused to utter a single word. He was sad and frightened. He hugged me tightly and said "I'm sorry" again and again. He asked me to marry him. I tried to smile and comfort him, "Harvey, it was not your fault."And I began to hum him some songs in the chill air. Suddenly sadness choked me. I burst into tears. He was so worried and begged me not to cry. He tried to cheer me up by singing me a very old song "*Night atthe Harbor*". He was so guilty that I pitied him. He never smiled after the strange love making. If it was such a sad thing, why did we make it? No, I wanted us to be happy. So I sung for him one after another. I could feel his loving eyes on my face when I was singing, but when I turned to look at him he would bend down humbly. It was about 2 o'clock in the early morning and freezing. He went to the street and brought back a plastic bag. He torn it open and put it on the brick I was sitting. Then he hugged me tightly under his shirt. I told him my childhood, my dear playmates at home and my families. He kissed me and told me his childhood. His family was poor. His parents were honest farmers. He didn't have as many friends as I did. He sounded so alone in the world. I couldn't help but being honest with such a boy. I told him about Clinton. He kissed me gently and smiled at my greediness. The night broke up at half past five in the morning. He found a stain of blood on his shirt and began to weep. He said I looked like a nun when he first saw me, but now I was a little woman. We took the bus to the university. I said "bye Harvey, be happy" at the parting cross. He said bye in a low voice and ran away. I walked slowly on the lonely and cold campus. My roommates were still sound asleep when I knocked at the door. No.8 opened the door. I took a basin, a towel and a thermos of hot water to the wash room and had a simple bath. Harvey called me when I was going to bed. He just called to make sure I was safe in the dorm. I told him to have a rest. His voice was small and sad.

When I got up, it was already time for lunch.

September 29

A large part of the day has passed. I spent most of the time sleeping. I asked Six to wake me up at 1 o'clock. Then when she left I fell asleep again. It was a guilty sleep. I kept thinking of study, opened my heavy eyes but fell asleep again. At half past two Six came back. She dragged me out of bed. I washed my face in cold water and went out to catch the last warmth of the sun. I was eager to fly and to shout into the vast sky.

September 30

Clinton wrote a letter to expose his fervent love for me. Well, too late, man. I've given you so many chances which you contemptuously regarded as childish. Now, you are too late for my love. The train has to start on time, leaving the late comers on the platform. I cried several teardrops for Clinton and went happily to hang around with Harvey.

October 3

Now Harvey is telling me his understanding of *Wuthering Heights*. He is not a very good organizer with words and tosses his head impatiently when I laugh at his clumsiness. Why does Heathcliff love Catherine so much? He is lonely. No one in the world loves him except Catherine. The tragedy is that Catherine chooses a wrong man as her husband. But why doesn't she marry the one she really loves? I am confused and tell Harvey so. He is satisfied with my confusion and pats me affectedly on my back. Then he falls asleep on the desk while I am still reading.

October 11

Ryan, Rebecca and I went to have a walk in the park today. I pretended to know the way, yet got us lost at first. We walked in a strange street where dustbins were so few. Ryan was holding his garbage all the way. I was touched and embarrassed. Finally we got to the park and had a good time there. Ryan showed us some French songs in his dorm which he shared with a Japanese student. Rebecca and I were whispering where to pee while Ryan was having a shower. We didn't know how to take our leave and shifted from one foot to the other. Thank God, Ryan came out quickly and told us to use his toilet while he went to the corridor to avoid the possible noise. We rushed in to relieve our swelling bellies and laughed and praised Ryan for his consideration. We were quite relaxed when he came back again. He told us something about the US and said the rich were getting richer while the poor getting poorer in this affluent country. I was surprised to know there were poor people in America and more surprised to know he had to earn his own tuition. His mother wanted to give him some money while his father objected. And, he could earn enough money for one year's stay in China! How I wish to travel around to see the world, to see Tower of London, to see romantic

Paris and energetic Africa. Let Echo be my guide.[5] She went to the Sahara desert with her Spanish husband and lived a bohemian life and wrote many fascinating stories. Let Echo be my guide to the paradise of freedom and the great beauty of nature.

October 15

I am happy now. I think I am changing for the better. My heart begins to warm up to love and it will miss Harvey from time to time. Unfortunately he doesn't seem to miss me at all. I force him to call me every Wednesday which he obeys after my vehement threats and sweet coaxing.

October 22

The class went to see a film while I had to stay to save 2 Yuan. The old clock on the city square is singing affectionately " the East is red with the rising sun, Chairman Mao was born in China" and then comes the ancient and nostalgic" dang, dang, dang, dang, dang, dang". It's six pm now. I am alone in the classroom to worship the unearthly beauty of the late afternoon sky. Big blocks of red, pink, and orange clouds are floating over trees and buildings.

October 28

Chrysanthemums are blooming in the cool autumn air. I picked one up on the way to my classroom and stuck it on the

---

5 Echo was a woman writer from Taiwan. She went to the Sahara Desert with her Spanish husband and wrote stories about their life there.

back wall. I wanted everyone to see its beauty and be happy. Some classmates laughed at my stupidity while teachers smiled to see a gold chrysanthemum when they looked up from their textbooks.

Yangzi is in low spirit again. Donald hasn't written to her for almost a month. She came here tonight with the old ones and asked me to translate every word to her, again. I did it and added something else to make her happy. What's wrong with Donald?

November 9

Rebecca and I invited Ryan to dinner. He caught a cold and had a running nose. He refused to eat the dish Rebecca specially ordered for him which almost brought her to tears. I didn't eat much either, watching the pure water coming out of his high nose, crossing his lips and dropping on the table. I wondered why he didn't wipe it up, yet I was not sure whether it was polite to remind him of its coming. So I sat there gazing at him which made him more agitated even than the chicken giblets Rebecca ordered for him.

November 17

Rebecca came to my dorm at noon. She brought me three bananas and asked me to call Ryan. No, I won't call him for anything! It takes me a year's courage and wisdom to communicate with a foreigner! I yelled in my mind but agreed to try and Rebecca left happily. Alas, what shall I do? I need to get myself drunk first with Maotai before I have the nerve to pick up the phone. Making ourselves understood by people from other cultures is harder than climbing the Everest!

November 20

My eyes are wet not with tears but with too much stress. I've used them for almost 20 hours. I spent the night admiring the bright moon with Harvey and tried in vain to seduce him. He called me yesterday after lunch but offended me for something I quickly forgot. He called me again after dinner and begged to see me at 9. I said no coldly, like a queen, and put down the receiver with great triumph, knowing surely that he would call again which he did within ten seconds. I was glad to have so much face before my roommates and agreed to see him. Then I washed my face with a dancing heart and went to study in the classroom. At 9 pm my desk mate told me somebody was waiting for me outside the classroom. I was so SURPRISED to find Harvey there grinning from ear to ear! He grabbed my arms and laughed at my pretentious surprise. We ran merrily downstairs and went to the bank of the golden river. The man-made river was still as dry as a desert. Withered leaves made a nice carpet for lover's feet. Harvey was too shy to take actions. So we just stood on the bank as silently as trees. No, my hilarious spirit won't bear such an insult. I began to provoke him with sharp questions to which he only gave a shrug and some theoretical answers. Pooh , such a log! My body was aching for his gentle touch, yet he was here playing with fallen leaves. I was so annoyed that I pushed him into the dry river and laughed. He was aroused, climbed up and hugged me affectionately. We kissed and hugged till the lights in the 8th dorm building were turned off one after another. Oh, I hated to leave him. So I lingered till all the lights were out and the gate was closed to me. Good, now that I can't enter the dorm we could spend the night together guiltlessly. We went to a tiny video room where many student lovers were pretending knights and beauties in private compartment. I wanted to have one of the compartments and be a seducing beauty but Harvey was too shy to be my knight. So we came out to the chilly air and wandered in the empty street. Then we came back to school and found shelter in the corridor of the school clinic. I told Harvey how I wanted to live always in the movies---no school, no competition, no rules, no discipline and I could be with him all the time. How I wish all my splendid dreams could be turned into reality with a blink of my curious eyes! My poor boy didn't comment on my wild talks. He stood quietly in the cold air. Maybe his mechanical brain did not work as well as mine. But he kissed me and wrapped me in his shabby jacket. I don't know whether we will have a future together but I do know I want to be sincere and kind to him. He's not talkative or romantic but he cares for me.

November 24

Tonight I went to Harvey's dormitory with Donna (No.7). His seven roommates were friendly and tried to make us feel at home. One of the boys played his two-stringed Chinese violin and others told many jokes to make us laugh. They were so kind. I wanted to repay their kindness in some way. I tried to be natural though my face was red and hot. It was my first time to be the center of so many friendly boys. Harvey was like a happy prince and walked us to building No.8 afterwards. He looked into my eyes and said,

"Your knees got periodic pain in cold weather; you'd better put on warm pants now." I smiled and said, Harvey, you are lovely. I couldn't tear myself away from him. I was feeling like there was no tomorrow when he ran away.

I begin to really like him.

December 14

I ate too much for lunch. I am a little tired now but I don't plan to have a nap. The memory of last weekend was so beautiful. I must write it down before its color fades away. Now I turn on the recorder and put on the earphone. Let time flow back to the beautiful Friday, wonderful Saturday and the romantic Sunday.

Walking around Zhengzhou city may be boring to other people. But when I walked with Harvey, the long way became sweet and short. We walked and talked, holding hands. My feet trembled with too much walking but I dragged on happily. Darkness made me gentle and lovely. I didn't have the heart to be harsh to him in the peaceful night. We wandered back to school and went to the sports ground where we had spent a night on the chairman's platform. I could still remember his sad and regretful eyes when I forced a mouthful of water into his throat and laughed at his obedience. He ran his arms around my waist with a metal column between us. When it got colder and colder, he found some newspapers and made me a little mattress on the chairman's platform. I fell asleep on the small mattress while he chased away mosquitoes for me. Now, we were here again. I happened to pick up a used newspaper and we sat on it. Again it was cold and blowing dust. He held me in his arms and gave me enough time to behave like a spoiled child or a proud queen. He smiled at my every little whim and kissed me. Though his kiss was as sweet as sunshine, I preferred putting my head over his shoulder. I was far away from reality, far away from my crazy dreams and was in a strange but comfortable state. He looked at his watch consistently to make sure that I wouldn't be late. He didn't want me to spend another night in the cold air. Then we had to say goodbye. O, I hated to part from him. I complained of headache and asked him to play basketball with me the next morning. He was concerned about my health and said firmly that I needed exercise. He would borrow a basketball and wake me up in the morning. With a clear vision of tomorrow I went to the dorm joyfully.

How should life be so lovely! I just came back from Harvey's audio-video classroom with No. 8.

Harvey invited me to attend his listening class. I asked little Eva (No. 8) to go with me since she was not in a good mood this weekend. Harvey led us to his classroom and sat down to write something on a card. I bent down to see what he was doing but he covered the card with both hands. Ahh, he was writing a Christmas card for me! Such a cute boy! After a while he gave it to me. It was a beautiful card with green pine trees and white snow on it. He wrote: my dear friend, I wish you have all the joys of the world and never cry a tear! Merry Christmas and Happy New Year! ----from the man who loves you. I was so happy even little Eva envied me.

Wasn't my weekend perfect?

December 22

I received a card from Ye. He was my desk mate in senior high school before we were separated to classes of science and art. I still remember one spring day when he called me secretly downstairs. I looked out of the window and found he was trying to throw a China rose to me. He knew I loved flowers and stole one for me from the garden. I was so surprised at his generosity for he was always making fun of me. Anyhow I was pleased at his kindness and tried to catch the rose on the second floor. Once, twice, ah, bad luck, I just couldn't catch it. He called me an idiot and ran up to thrust the red rose in my hand. How time flies! I am not that "idiot" and innocent girl any more. And where is he? He didn't even write his address on the envelope. He didn't want me to find him. Why? I miss him so much.

Rebecca keeps urging me to call Ryan. I have to continue the cultural shock in my own country. How easy it would be to give up this tiring communication, but it is not my nature to leave things half done. I have to be the tiresome bug that tries to jump across two worlds.

Yangzi came to see me in the evening and insisted on buying me a little toy bear as a Christmas gift. I took it to the dorm where it won the hearts of the girls immediately. It was passed on from hand to hand while I went to the classroom. There I found another card on my desk. It was from Zeng, another desk mate in senior high school. He called me his sister and accompanied me to see the doctor when I caught a fever one winter. Now he is at another college in Zhengzhou. Hope to see him soon. How lucky for me to have so many good friends! I was encouraged by the strength and beauty of friendship and called Ryan. Alas, language was still a problem. I couldn't express myself well in English and finished the conversation in despair.

December 27

So went Christmas! Yangzi came here in the afternoon with a new letter from Donald. I translated his love for her and she left as happy as a lark. I pray everything would go smoothly with them.

January 19

"*The song of silence*" was ringing in my head while I was spending a silent afternoon in the classroom. I called Harvey after class but he was not in the dorm so I went to see the doctor alone. How I need him when I am sick. I feel so lonely and weak. Yet he seldom calls me these days. I begin to doubt whether he cares me at all. Maybe I have to say goodbye to him sooner or later. I've tried not to think of him but Turning has imprinted his picture in my swirling head. Where are you now? How hard it is when we have to stride alone toward an unknown future!

January 22

Harvey came to see me at my call. We stood speechless by the bank of the dry river. It seemed that we had nothing to say to each other. A great torrent of happiness or sorrow had to come to a sudden standstill in front of "a machine". When he refused to be aroused by my sharp words, I came back to the classroom. He is too young and too simple to know the sweetness of affection.

January 23

I hoped Harvey would call me after lunch but he didn't. I stayed in the dorm chatting and laughing while my heart was aching for his call. The phone did not ring so I had to go to the classroom. Oh, I didn't want to study. The way to the classroom was so lonely. I dragged on this lonely road and became sadder and sadder when my hate for him grew stronger and stronger. Harvey was a fool! I hated him! I despised him! How dare he keep silent when I wanted to hang out with him! I sat on my seat by the window and urged the sun to set quickly so that I could see Harvey. I didn't know whether I missed him or not but I wanted to be with him and out of this classroom. He is still a child and does not have strong feelings for people. He hurts me with his indifference. I will leave him alone to grow up and will never speak to him. Harvey, you are disappointing! Tears poured down my face. It has been a long time since I cried. I make up my mind to surrender to Abraham who is so in love with me but, it is not right. I know it is not right. I am still innocent and na?ve. I can't be angry with anyone long. Life is so wonderful. If anger walks into my heart I will surely feel cold and lonely. No, it is not my nature. I am an optimistic horse. I gallop to sunshine and grassland without hesitation. Don't sigh when you are troubled. Maybe the bad thing turns out to be a blessing in disguise. I used to ridicule those who are interested in empty talks. Not now. I find life has to be a waste from time to time. When I feel confined to a desolate island I choose stupidity and talk merrily about nothing with nobody. Nothing is important now. I sit grimly by the window and make friends with darkness.

January 25

After the extensive reading exam I felt strangely sick and sad. I miss Harvey but he never calls me. I hate him and this hatred spoiled the exam. I am so disappointed with Harvey, with myself and with the world. How I wish to find somebody rich so that I can quit the time consuming school life and do what I really want to do. I am so tired to strive. How I need a rich and kind man to help me out of this miserable life! It's so difficult to be a human being. I'd rather be a bird if I have the chance to see the Creator. Life is so short yet I have to waste so much time in obeying some stupid rules and in book reciting and competition for scholarships. Who will take me to the paradise of freedom?

January 26

How time flies when love is with me! Harvey is a magician. He made me cry bitterly last night and laugh merrily today.

Last night should have been a nice one but we ruined it. Harvey called in the afternoon and we made an appointment at 9 p.m. I came back from the classroom earlier and washed my face for this big occasion. My heart was singing yet my face was stern. I shouldn't be happy, for he had disappointed me these days. Yet I couldn't help feeling good on the way downstairs. There he was, smiling ear to ear. Seeing me coming he took out a red red apple from his pocket. His small eyes were glistering with obvious happiness that I felt self-conscious under his gaze. He studied me for a moment and whispered that I was as beautiful as the bright moon. Yes, there was a full moon above the trees. It was beautiful. I was like the moon? Well, you made me so, Harvey. I was so relaxed and girlish when I was with him. I forgot all my hatred at the sight of him. We sat on the dry grass by the bank with me eating the delicious apple while he studied me with his glistering eyes. He said he couldn't wait to kiss me and kissed me gently on my cheek. He said it was too cold for a girl to sit on the ground and picked me up into his laps and hugged me tightly. I felt like a little darling girl and was moved. He suggested us staying the whole night in building No.19 since we would part soon for the winter vacation. I hesitated but still went back to the dorm to fetch my scarf. I had heard that there were two students found dead in that half deserted building two years ago. I was scared and suggested not to go there. Suddenly he changed his mood and the gentle glow on his face was gone. He looked like a ghost and urged me to go back. I was so terrified but still tried to smile. How I wanted to be with him? Yet he had turned his back to me. I asked him why not walk me to the dorm. He said proudly that he only came here to give me the apple, nothing more. Alas, how dare he say such cruel words when I was still so attached to him? My roommates were surprised to find me back. I answered briefly "that guy is disgusting!" and lay down on the bed. I was hot with anger and pulled only one quilt to cover myself. Pressing my toy bear to my face I sobbed hysterically. Tears ran down my temple across my hair and sunk into the pillow. My roommates tried to comfort me. They patted me lightly on my cheek which that disgusting boy had just kissed. I forced a smile to them and closed my eyes. I switched the channel of the radio but couldn't find a pleasant one. The telephone rang. I lay still. Eva answered it. It was Harvey. I asked her to hung up on him but she wouldn't. I got up and smashed the phone on him. Before I could reach the bed it rang again. I picked up. "Why are you not happy?" he asked cautiously. "I am sleeping!"A short pause. "Are you angry with me?" he asked innocently. "Definitely!" I yelled, right hand resting on my hip. "I was hesitating when you went for the scarf. The building is haunted and you still have one exam to prepare. So I urged you to go back."He said kindly. I kept silent. It was not my turn to find words this time. After a long pause he said coaxingly, "Go to bed, ok?" I put down the receiver quickly and went to bed. This time I pulled up another quilt for I felt cold now that the anger had gone. Actually I knew Harvey was right. I felt guilty to make him unhappy when he was at the height of his happiness. I cried again, not for me but for poor Harvey.

I got up late this morning and went to the classroom after a luxurious breakfast in the best cafeteria. I studied calmly and efficiently. When I was tired I would walk out of the classroom and think about Harvey's gentle kiss and happy eyes. He called again after lunch. "Why were you so angry last night?"I didn't answer but introduced another topic, "Do you still have some apples?" "No, I gave them all to my friends." Then my roommates broke in, "Harvey, we want to eat your apples!" they shouted jokingly and snatched the receiver from me. I can't conceal my smile anymore. When the receiver finally passed to me I asked him to buy some apples for the girls. "Of course!" he answered happily, "study hard for the exam little girl, I will call you tonight." My heart was bursting with love and happiness. I couldn't help laughing out when we were going upstairs. Donna thought I was making fun at her and ran into the classroom and locked the door on me.

January 27

Darkness, mysterious night. Harvey, why are you so dear to me? You are so pure. How I wanted to be part of you when you told me how you loved to stand by the river watching the rain pouring down and to play hide –and- seek in the peach orchard in April when rosy cheeks of little girls made a perfect picture among the pink flowers. I have found a pure and noble heart under your shabby clothes. My heart bloomed when you whispered "marry me". No one has been so true to me. When I was a little farmer's girl strolling along the country road, somewhere there was a boy watching silently from a distance. When I was chatting with my playmates under a starry night, somewhere there was a boy sitting in the dark thinking of me. Harvey, we have shared so many things since a long time ago though we only knew each other last year. I pray this beautiful feeling we experienced last night would last forever. Harvey, I am sorry for my nasty behavior the night before last. He said after I went angrily upstairs he was lost for a while not knowing what happened. He went to stand by the bank and fought his tears back. Poor boy, my dear boy, I made you unhappy on your birthday. How can I make it up for you? I am always afraid that some unexpected things would happen and now it really happened. It can't be predicted because neither of us are prophets. It can't be avoided because I am so stubborn and you are so silly. Well I can only comfort myself by believing that life is full of trials and holds many surprises. You went back and dialed my number. The line was busy and you couldn't reach me at first. When you finally reached me half an hour later I hung up on you without a word. Harvey, last night you said regretfully that it was all your fault. No, it was also my fault. Oh, Harvey, I'm sure there are still many surprises ahead to make up for the disappointment, sadness and even despair. I'm willing to endure all these and bring you as much happiness as possible.

January 28

I'm alone in the classroom now. We will have the last exam of this semester tomorrow and will be liberated for the winter vacation. With the exams drawing to an end I become aimless.

I spent a crazy night with Harvey in building No.18. We made love on the concrete floor of an empty and dusty classroom. There is no mystery between us now. I don't want to know it was right or wrong. I called Harvey but he was out. He called me twice when I went for lunch. I was uneasy without seeing him since the brisk parting in the morning. My chest is aching periodically. There is blood coming down from my nose. I am quite frightened. What will happen to me?

Yangzi invited me and Donna to a nice dinner and gave me ten Yuan afterwards for me to buy some snacks. I bought some cakes and shared with Donna. Little Donna saved a few in the bag and whispered to me that they were for Harvey. I was touched by her consideration. Thank you Donna for liking the one I like.

The score for intensive reading has come out. Mine is very low. What's wrong with my studying method? I've worked so hard yet still get such a poor score. Why? I played truant on intensive reading class but wasn't it a waste of time? I felt much more rewarded in reading original novels than listening to his mechanical explanation of old and useless texts.

How silly am I to expect a high score when the function of the exam is to test our memory of what the teacher said exactly in class! Ok, I can't get the first scholarship. So what? I just can't have my flying wings and open arms tied by irresponsible teachers and out of date textbooks. I pray that some miracle would happen to show me another way to fulfill my dream.

January 31

I wanted to go home but Yangzi wished me to stay in Zhengzhou a little longer. Donald had been silent for more than two months. She was so sad that I did not have the heart to leave her like this.

Clinton is here with me now. He was foolish enough to force his love on me last night. I couldn't refuse him when he was so emotional and excited. So I rolled with him on the grassland. I was trying not to laugh at his clumsy and artificial expression of love. Gosh, he copied everything from books! Didn't he have any natural feelings? He held me in his arms, fell down to the grassland and then rolled together! It was a typical show of stupid love movies. I was embarrassed at his plagiarism yet pitied him when he put my hand to his fast beating heart. God, I don't know what I am doing now. I am crazy. I hope to start a new life as soon as possible.

Chapter Six

The Last Dance

February12

Now I'm really at home. Mother is washing the dishes. Father is watching TV. My little nephew is running from room to room. I'm happy and tired. Father has decided to clean the market to earn money. He told mother he felt so piteous riding around to sell bean curd. How I want to pay their silent love back! Patricia, you must be very clear that you have a noble cause on your shoulder. I should make this vacation a happy and meaningful one.

February 13

I don't want to get up though I'm completely awake. I'm lazy but there are so many things waiting for me. I think of Harvey. I am not sure about our future. What I need are feelings but he can only give me body because he has given his affection to another girl who stole his heart in a peach orchid. There is no pure and sweet memory behind us. He told me after one love making that I was ordinary-looking. If he marries me, he would be relieved to leave me alone at home. If he marries a beautiful girl, she may flirt with other men. Gosh, I may appreciate his other merits but never this one. He is so traditional even ridiculous. I'm disappointed at his philosophy on love. I couldn't bear his keeping another girl in his mind when he told me "I love you".

When I came back from the village fair I found my second sister lying in bed. I asked her if she believed in "love". Sorry, I made a mistake. I "wanted" to ask her but I also found a distance between us. It's the first time I am aware of her love for my brother-in-law. I am eager to go back to school. My parents are very kind to me but I am out of place at home. I want to study. I want to fly. I want to see the world.

February 14

It's about half past four in the early morning. I am frightened by the total darkness and silence and woke up completely. All of a sudden Father's digital watch announced the time. A chill ran through my body. Why am I a coward? This strange fear of darkness has sunk deeper and deeper in my heart since I was left to "watch the door" in my childhood when other members of the family went to the field. I lay in bed as still as possible in case some ghost would snatch me if I moved.

I bought two bunches of plastic roses yesterday. I gave them to Father and let him give them to Mother as Valentine gifts. He agreed happily. His love for Mother is so natural and strong that I envy Mother. Where is my lover?

The day begins to break. I become relaxed and turn on the

tape recorder. I am listening to the thirteen theme songs from *Dream in the Red Chamber* and seventeen English songs from *"Now that's what I call love"*. I like the Chinese songs because they are slow, subtle and sad. I also like the English songs because they are almost the opposite of the Chinese ones. It seems that people in the west live as innocently and happily as children. I wonder how they do it.

February 15

Tonight is Chinese New Year's Eve. I've been in high spirit since I came back home. Yet with the spring festival coming near I began to feel sorry for Yangzi. She begged me to stay at a friend's rented house for 10 days and cried when I had to come home for the festival. She was so lonely. Donald hadn't written her a letter for a long time. I was so worried about her that I dreamed of Donald last night. He stood under a splendid flower tree and told me his longing for Yangzi. I was touched and ran to tell her the good news but couldn't find her. I was busy putting new pictures on the wall the whole day and did not call her. I hope everything is fine with her.

Mother came in to give me 50 Yuan as the New Year's gift. We Chinese call it "press age money". Children are given this kind of money so that they can grow up quickly though the literal meaning of the money is not letting the age grow bigger. I am one year older now with the "press age money". I'm twenty two years old! Ahh, as fresh as a China rose yet as confused as a sphinx. I'd like to make New Year's resolutions now.

First, I hope Clinton can have a successful year. I promise I will never hurt him that much. He behaved like being madly in love with me when I stayed in Zhengzhou for the extra 10 days. He bought me the most expensive rose named "archbishop" and wrote me a six–page love letter. O, poor man, why are you so late? I tried not to look at his piteous eyes when I refused his rose and his letter. So the first New Year's good wish goes to Clinton---the late lover.

Second, I hope and pray that Harvey can love me solely. He was sick during my stay in Zhengzhou. I went to his dorm to see him and found he was writing something in a diary. I snatched it and read his feelings for another girl. I threw his diary and ran hysterically downstairs. He ran with me and wrestled to let me calm down. He said I misunderstood him. Well, how shall I understand him correctly when he cheated me so? But he was terribly sick and looked so helpless. I made up with him though my heart was so unwilling. Now the New Year has come. Harvey, let's be good friends at least.

Third, I will work hard and make conspicuous progress in English. I will have to find a part-time job to earn my tuition for Grade three. I want a guitar and a camera.

Fourth, I hope all the people who care for me will have their dreams realized in the New Year.

At exactly 12 o'clock the audience on the CCTV shouted "过年啦"(Happy New Year). Tears sting my eyes. Happy New Year to you, Yangzi! Wish you have lots of letters from Donald this year. Happy New Near to you, Harvey!

I promise myself that I would be more successful and happy in 1999.

February 16

I slept lightly and was excited with fireworks "bibibaobao" the whole night. I used to get up early to show off my new clothes. Not now. I haven't bought any new clothes for the Spring Festival since I went to senior high school. All the families have been saving for my tuition. I do not have the heart to buy new things for myself. Father would sigh when I put on my old clothes for the New Year. To make him less guilty I put on my new school uniform one time. Last year he insisted on buying me a new jacket. It was bright pink with yellow cartoons on it. O, father, you still thought I was your baby girl? I was so embarrassed to wear it in front of my playmates who were wearing suits and boots then. However, I put it on happily and took a photo in it. But with me going to college, the condition is getting worse with my family. The four thousand Yuan tuition each year is like a stone rolling on father's back and it will roll and roll for four years. He still makes and sells Tofu, raises pigs, plows fields and this year he has to bribe someone so that he can be a cleaner for the village fair. O, dear God, please help us in some way. At least please help me to show my gratitude and love to father. He shouldn't feel guilty at all. He has tried his best as a Chinese farmer and he doesn't deserve my harsh words and cold eyes! Yes, I will get up, put on my old clothes and have the New Year's morning jiaozi as happily as a princess.

When we are still having jiaozi, kinsmen begin to come to Kowtow. They come in three or five and kneel down before the ancestor's wooden tablets in the middle room. The first one for general greeting, the second one for my dead grandparents on father's side, the third one for father and mother then they stand up, one hand covering the other and raise the hands for another general greeting. Mother has already spread a mat on the floor but if there are too many people at a time the younger ones would kneel on the bare floor and have a patch of dirt on their new pants. After all the greetings to the dead and the living, they would turn to speak with Father. Usually father would offer cigarettes to men, delicacies to teenagers and little token of "press age money" to children. They would accept it after protesting for a while. Then they leave and another group would come and the same thing happens again. While father and mother are busying with all these New Year greetings, I go out to see Ping. Before Ping and Qin were married they would always come to see me on New Year's morning. Now Ping is engaged to a man who agrees to marry into her family since her parents do not have a boy to pass on the family name. When a man is married into a girl's family, their children must use the mother's surname. It's considered a great shame for the man's family if he marries into a girl's family. So men do not do this unless they are really poor or do not have a family. It's said that Ping's fiancé is a tramp whose parents are divorced which is regarded as a tragedy in the countryside. A boy with divorced parents is pitied as an orphan and is encouraged to marry into a girl's family. I am eager to see this boy who is going to marry my prettiest girl friend Ping. Unfortunately he is too shy to come out. So I asked Ping out. We went to see Qin who was now married and lived in another village. My dearest Qin was so happy to see us. She showed us all her new things and insisted that we should sit on her new bed. Her husband was eager to please us now that his bride was happy. He treated us with lots of delicacies. His mother came over to greet us. On the first look I knew Qin had a challenging mother-in-law. Her face was smiling yet her eyes were suspicious. I felt a chill running through my body unconsciously. While her husband was preparing lunch Qin had an intimate talk with us. She said she was very sad in heart. She married Hong while she was still in love with another boy. She wouldn't have done so if her father hadn't spent the entire 6,000 Yuan dowry gift. She was forced to marry. Fortunately Hong was a nice man. She said he was very kind to her and she would try to love him now that she was his wife. Well, life can't be predicted nor planned. Expected things happen only when it is very sure. But what can be sure when life is such a mystery? After lunch we said goodbye to a tearful Qin and went dancing in a small disco at the end of our village. There I met the boys who had learned dancing from Qin and the boy I had had a crash on since I was born. We felt excited and safe with each other's presence yet did not talk. It is a rule in the countryside that boys and girls should not talk or dance together otherwise they would be gossiped within ten minutes. Qin challenged this feudal idea once and danced with the boys. She was ridiculed and despised by the stupid villagers who wouldn't have their daughters talk to her any more. I love her more for this. She would always be the purest and bravest girl in my heart. She was my friend who let me warm my cold hands under her coat, she was my sister who stole her grandma's money to buy me food, and she was my comrade who defended me when I was called a thief for stealing sweet potatoes in the field. O, Qin, you were my queen who led us charge to the top of the hill where I was so willing to present a bunch of wild chrysanthemum to you. I sat in the flickering neon light and thought of Qin. God, I kneel on my knees to pray for her. Let her have a loving husband and a happy life.

February 18

It's windy today. Father and mother have gone to see my grandparents as the custom goes. On the first day after the spring festival the married daughter should "go to mother's house" with her husband. So I am alone at home to finish translating Donald's old love letter for Yangzi. They are making up a fairy tale. I pray that this kind of love really exists and I will be encouraged and enlightened by the most beautiful thing in the world. I also want to see with my own eyes that pure love leads to a happy marriage.

February 20

I dreamed that I was at school, busy and active. Then I turned on the tape recorder and listened to *Gone with the Wind* which reminded me of Mr. Turning strangely. Like Harvey I keep another man in my heart so we are fair now.

I must do things like an adult next semester.

I wanted to take a picture and let Harvey keep it around his neck like westerners do, but was discouraged when I looked myself in the mirror in the Photoshop. I had to leave without my picture being taken.

The sky is more blue and the moon brighter here in the countryside than in big cities. I wish I could share this beautiful scene with Harvey. I murmured to myself: the cool moon light, the gentle breeze and the leafless trees are all to Harvey's liking. Yes, distance makes the heart grow fonder. My heart bursts with love this winter vacation. I bought two bunches of roses for mother, cut the roses out of the old pictures and put it on the wall near my bed. I call my little niece Rose. How in love am I!

February 23

I am in a good mood now. I sang and danced with my childhood friend Ping and her sister Mai who had been accepted into our "three gangs" since she graduated from junior high school. It was really nice. Qin came home yesterday. We went to the field to pick wild vegetables as we did more than a decade ago. We went to trace our childish pleasure and the lost youth. We sat on the green carpet of wheat. O, God, where are the two girls who used to covet every leaf and every fruit of the field? Where are the two dirty and naughty little girls who used to catch crickets while my black cow was grazing the tender grass? Where are they, my dear Lord? They are here sitting on patches of wheat and talking about sad love stories. Qin is never content with her marriage. I don't know how to comfort her. Things done can't be undone.

What else can she do except to forget all her ambitious dreams and be a dutiful farmer's wife? Life is so hard for us. She married the man for that little money which was squandered by her father. And my brother, he even thought of selling his second daughter for some badly needed money. Look at his face, what a face is it! So helpless, so worried, so sad! How I wish to help you my dear brother! Yet, what can I do? The whole family bet on me. I am their star that shines in the darkest night. I do not talk much at home. My stone face covers a bleeding heart. I won't let myself be discouraged by the pitiful situation. I will laugh and dance and be as happy as everybody else. Yet, I would crucify myself if I can't fulfill my family's ambitious dreams for me. I will work hard, I will have a position in this society, I will earn trucks and trucks of money to spread to the needy hands, and I will burn myself to give light and warmth to those who are as honest and helpless and dear as Qin and my brother.

I must change and make a great leap forward next semester. I must fill my empty head with as much knowledge as possible.

May God be with me! Sweet dream to all my friends!

February 24

We four went dancing tonight. I couldn't bear seeing my friends disappointed, so I took a deep breath and invited them to dance when we reached the end of the village at our walk. I spent 8 Yuan for a last happy night with my playmates. Totally worth it. When I walked down the spiral stairs of the dancing room I thought of "*the last waltz*". Yes, it would be the last time for us to be together. I would go back to school, Qin would go to her new home, Mai and Ping would go to the city and be farmer workers. However, I still felt a little guilty. I could spend the money in a more useful way. I could buy something for my parents who have been saving every cent for my tuition. I heard them discussing how to give me a treat before I leave for school. Mother suggested buying me 2 Yuan sweet dumplings and father agreed without hesitation. I should have stayed with them at home instead of dancing. Mother had asked me again and again to sit by her. I refused her coldly. I was so cruel and rude to my parents. I am so bad. I should work hard and be successful. May God bless my family. I will get up early tomorrow morning to clean the house and be kind to my parents.

Chapter Seven

Enchanted on the Ghost Day

March 1

Where am I? Can you guess? Yes, in my classroom! I'm fresh and energetic. How wonderful to see so many young faces again! How wonderful to speak English again!

March 3

I hang out with Harvey and fastened a loose button on his shirt for him. It was a typical scene in Chinese love movies: fasten his button, smile at him shyly and smell his body while biting off the thread. Pooh, I was amused by my clumsy imitation and thought of Clinton's rolling on the grass.

March 6

I'm reading *The Thorn Birds* now. I haven't finished my homework but a novel is more attractive than textbooks.

Clinton came to see me this noon. I was moved by his strong attachment to me and prepared a bottle of milk for his journey to

Tianjin where he would borrow some money from his aunt.

Harvey is here in the classroom. I showed him a long letter I wrote to him when at home and the long letter Clinton wrote to me last winter. I can't predict what he will say about it. He is still reading while I am thinking of a part-time job.

March 7

I was terribly disappointed when Harvey did not say a single word about the two letters. He did not say anything about my love for him. He was a stone, refused to be moved. I felt lost at his indifference.

I went to the people's park alone and came back to listen to the sad symphony and felt like crying. I gave my boys away one after another. Now I was left alone and lost. I hope some knight would appear before my expecting eyes.

Forget about boys! I should be crazy about English. I must make great progress so that I can fly away from this stale place. I hate routines. I need someone to love me and guide me. I am easily tired of things. I hoped to be a cheerful girl when I got to school, but a week had passed without me making any study plans and being happy. I need a part-time job so badly. How can I be cheerful without money and boys! I'm hungry for a real and strong love. Who can give it to me? Not Harvey. He is too young to read my heart and too slow to catch up with my tempo.

Good night all the people who care about me.

Good luck Patricia!

March 8

I am reading *The Thorn Birds* most of the day and wonder what kind of country is Australia.

I am curious about what will happen if I call Harvey. Damn it, he is never active. I am so impatient. If only I can control my curiosity and kindness! I need money to buy a guitar. I need more than one way to let my saturated feelings loose.

March 12

There was an English Corner tonight in front of the classroom building. There were more students due to the appearance of four Americans. We were so eager to speak English, to know the outside world, to express ourselves that we almost suffocated the four creatures by surrounding them one layer after another. I listened excitedly and put in my small voice nervously. How could they be so nice! They seemed to know our hearts. They looked kindly around to let us see their colorful eyes. How wonderful it would be to live with these friendly people who looked so gentle and friendly! Well, it is so easy for westerners to come to China but only the really rich Chinese can go abroad. It's so discouraging for common Chinese. It's a shame. It seems that the west world values money more than anything else.

March 14

I read the *21st century* newspaper and get to know that women's ideal lifestyle has changed greatly. They begin to have own their career and their secret to success is one word:

perseverance. Yes, women just can't put all their eggs in one basket of men. See what Yangzi is suffering now. She shouldn't depend on Donald for a living. She has to live a frugal and piteous life now that Donald won't send her money any more. Women just can't trust men whole-heartedly. We should earn our own living. God, please bless Yangzi. She is greedy but still lovely.

March 15

I tire myself with meaningless things. I look up words in the thick dictionary, copy beautiful sentences, recite Shelley's *Ode to the West wind* which I can't understand clearly, and listen to Liyang's crazy English. How I wish to have a quick leap forward after so many chores. I can't be a good farmer. I count the days of harvesting once I spread the seeds in the field. I am too impatient. If Chairman Mao is still alive, I will respond to his call and "rush to Communism".

March 16

I am too active for a pensive Harvey. It's a rule acknowledged throughout China that girls shouldn't be active. We must wait for the men to act and to make phone calls while the girl must pretend to care nothing about the boy though she may cry her eyes out for him. I am a wild horse. I can't wait, neither can be active so I have forced Harvey to call me every Wednesday. I was excited the whole morning. Then he called after lunch. We did not have much to say and hung up within 2 minutes.

I went to the classroom afterwards and found to my

astonishment that the cover of my *Longman Dictionary of Contemporary English* was broken! I was so sorry for this expensive and useless thing.

March 19

Ah, it was snowing! I screamed with my roommates for a while and walked to the library with my hands reaching out for the pure little darlings from Heaven.

March 20

It is a wonderful day today. The snow is melting and the air is as fresh as fresh can be. My heart is bursting with a true love for nature and life.

It's evening now. Harvey has come to study with me in my classroom. He taught Monitor a lesson with sharp and scornful words just now when the latter tried to ridicule his shortness. I was so proud of him. He was my Beowulf against the human-monster Monitor. Hah ha-ha, I was so happy when the monster slipped away, mourning his own uselessness.

March 21

I'm a strong girl. I came out of that terrifying love story with Monitor by kicking and screaming. I cried a million times, complained to my friends, wrote it out to the publishers and then found my Beowulf---Harvey--- to be my body and spiritual guard. What about those who are not as strong as me, who do not complain but keep sadly silent, who could not let steam off by writing, and who aren't lucky enough to find their Beowulf? I hear girls weeping at corners and in darkness. I see sorrows on their wretched faces. Not only premature love is bothering young souls but also poverty. Many of my friends pay their tuition with borrowed money. Just imagine under how much pressure we are living! Ben used to wrap himself with the classroom curtain to keep warm in cold winter. He eats the leftovers of other students. He stays in the classroom day and night, reading and writing. He is despised by his rich roommates. How should these students let steam off? I have been tortured by not being able to help them. I think and think and have a good idea. Yes, I could set up a hot-line with the phone in the dorm. I will ask all my roommates to participate in this organization. We will provide understanding and encouragement to people through a hot-line. Wow, we would all be anchor women. I told my ideas to my roommates. They all applauded and agreed to have a try. We discussed it and unanimously decided "Say you say me" would be a perfect name for our program. Then came the most exciting part. We chose ourselves beautiful and artistic names such as "soothing heart", "white dove" and "gentle singer". Then each of the anchor girls offered a motto of her own making on our pamphlet. How nervous and proud were we when our "Say you say me" came out of the printer. Yet I had to calm down to think of the next step when they left for the classroom after laughing and joking. I knew quite well that to set up the program was just a starting point. How should we understand and comfort the callers? How should we utter soothing words without being too weak and na?ve? What shall we do if some bad eggs call and make fun of us on purpose? How much do my roommates share my seriousness about this "huge" thing? They were too shy even to spread the pamphlets. They started to shrink when the idea came out as a fact. How far can "Say you say me" go?

March 22

Donna, Eva (No.8) and I stuck our pamphlets around the campus last night. Some boys whistled while reading our mottos and attractive names. We were a little bit nervous under their suspicious scrutiny. Two of the girls gave up already. I found one pamphlet we stuck on the wall near the dining hall lying on the ground and stamped by the passing feet. My roommates looked almost ashamed while my heart was sickening. After lunch one other girl gave up.

March 23

The phone rang. Gosh, our first caller! We sat on our bed looking at each other, not ready for the atomic bomb yet. Finally I got up and picked up the receiver, "Hello, May I help you?""Yes, who is the gentle singer? By the way, what is the purpose of this program? Hahaha...."the boy on the other end of the phone laughed weirdly. I recognized his voice at once. He was Monitor. How dare he talk like this! He knew the gentle singer was his girlfriend. I passed the phone on to her and they chatted and then she went out to have her date, forgetting all about the program.

March 24

Tonight was the second night since the birth of our hot-line. While we were still washing our dishes the phone rang. Donna picked it up. It was another boy from our class. He was curious about the artistic names. I urged Donna to hang up on such a mischievous call and waited professionally for a quality caller. Alas, "Say you say me" ended its short life with the first real call! When the poor boy asked Donna who she was, she answered laughingly, "Who do you think I am?" The boy took it as a flirt and hung up. That was it.

March 27

To earn some money I went to do a market survey for a mobile company. I knocked at strangers' doors one by one and smiled my most innocent smile to suspicious eyes. I walked into unfamiliar communities and was shouted out by fierce gatekeepers. I felt so oppressed, hurt and sadly tired. I swear to find a rich husband who can liberate me from worries for money so that I may have time and mood to appreciate the beauty of being alive. How I wish to do the thing I like instead of running here and there only for a mouth and a stomach.

There is a training class for Chinese painting. I will go to enroll my name for it tomorrow.

March 28

Rebecca was angry with me last night. I forgot our appointment with Ryan and went to "seek pleasure" with Harvey.

It was my second time to forget about them. Making friends with Chinese is easier than with foreigners so my mind chose the easier thing to do. However, I felt very sad when Rebecca told me Ryan would leave China in May. Sorry, man, I shouldn't break our promises. Rebecca was astonished to know that I spent so much time with boyfriends. Pooh, hang all the boys! They are dirty and stupid! How can you be such a fool to play with them? She was so angry that I felt ashamed of myself. I dropped my head and promised her never "indulge myself in love affairs". With her vehement attack in mind I went to bed cold and tired.

I called Ryan this noon. He was happy to receive my phone call and told me he would leave China in about five weeks. Suddenly I felt so sorry for the whole thing: the 100 times visits Rebecca and I paid to him; the many nervous phone calls I made with eyes closed; Ryan's patience and generosity; our hanging around together; his genuine relief when he found me among the crowd in one of the English Corners, and, O, my neglect of two appointments and their disappointment. We all have tried very hard to break the barriers of language and culture to know each other. It is so new and hard for each of us. At last when we begin to trust each other, Ryan's time in China is numbered.

Though Rebecca's long face is still fearful in my mind, I called Harvey again and went to the People's park with him. Sorry, Rebecca, this is me. I like boys. I like the freedom and relaxation which boys not girls can share with me. We walked aimlessly on dry grassland. I thought of Helen Keller's *Three days to see*, felt my way in the darkness and opened my eyes again gratefully to a bright and beautiful world. O, God, I love this world where so much pleasure and beauty are touching my every sense. I didn't know whether we were killing our precious time or not, yet I felt so right. However, dear Rebecca's long face flashed in front of my eyes. I dragged Harvey out of the Park quickly and went back to school. We shared a bowl of noodle in a small restaurant at the corner of the north gate. Neither of us wanted to say goodbye. So I went to the dorm, took my sword and ran to the grassland by the bank with Harvey. I decided to show him my shadow sword in the moon light. You see, I am not wasting time. I am doing exercise! I whispered to Rebecca's long face. I was greatly relieved when she faded away, smiling. Taking a deep breath, eyes half closed, feet apart, I began to move gracefully with my shining sword. Left, right, pause, sliding down, upright, I was a dancing spirit in the gentle moon light. I was intoxicated! I was beautiful! Harvey clapped his hand joyfully. "Terrific!" somebody else shouted. We looked around and found a man in military uniform sitting in the tall grass. He greeted us friendly and praised my sword dancing. He said I looked so unreal----red jacket, white pants, shining sword and filmy moonlight. I thanked him and we three sat in a group to chat. He said he was a soldier and lived with his grandma since his parents were divorced. He told us his adventures with five wolves in a mountain. His description was so vivid and he even stood up to perform his great art of wolf fighting. I laughed and giggled and stamped my feet till Harvey gave me a hint to behave myself. The wolf fighter then told us about his grandma who was very lonely and sad since she was abandoned even by her own daughter. He looked after her with his scanty salary. I asked him whether he was worried about money. He said no. He was quite content to live a simple life with his grandma. Well, he was different. Harvey was captured by his brave deeds and kind heart that he offered to see him off when we said goodbye. He forgot to kiss me and ran away with the hero.

March 29

March is here with sprouting buds and strong wind. Clinton has invited me to fly kites in his university founded by a Taiwanese and located in the countryside. I will think about it.

Every day when I open my eyes, the world reveals to me a new face. How miserable life would be in a world without light, sound or words! I couldn't hold my tears when Helen fought madly in a dark and mute world. I sat in my seat sobbing while Amy was showing us Helen's life on TV. O, the living creatures, let us treasure what we've got and be grateful.

I enrolled my name in a painting class this afternoon. I want to learn Chinese painting. This time I will keep it a secret. I am afraid I will be a laughing stock if I share my adventures with others. See what happened with the "Say you say me" program! After the first real call which was ruined by Donna's innocent flirtation, there appeared on the wall of men's dormitory a big paper warning the male comrades against Patricia Liu who was "trying desperately to find a boyfriend"! I was having the intensive reading class when Ben came up to me and said angrily about the wallpaper. I was enraged and terrified. How could people be so malicious? Who did it? Why? No one answered my questions nor called our hot-lines ever after.

April 1

I was a big fool on April Fool's Day. I did not want to waste the golden morning time listening to the teacher's nonsense at extensive reading class so I decided to go to the library. On the way to the library I realized that I did not have the card with me. Then I went to the dorm but I had the wrong key! At last I had to go to the classroom. What a Fool's Day!

Well, I can always see the positive side of life. My seat is my favorite place in the classroom. I like sitting there reading in the sun. I borrowed a novel named *Great Marie* this morning. If I can't be confident in the real world, I hide myself in an unreal one. All the novels reveal to me a splendid picture of the western world.

April 8

We will have Amy's oral class after a while. It is my turn to give a two-minute speech. I am not well prepared and sit nervously in my seat under the sun.

I insisted on putting Titanic pictures on the back wall of the classroom. Some students laughed and said it was not suitable for classroom. I don't know why. Here comes Amy.

April 10

Suddenly I miss Ryan very much. He will leave in May.

There are only a few weeks left now. I feel so sad. I wish he would kiss me on my cheek or hug me when he leaves as the western people always do. I went down stairs to call him but he was not in. Rebecca, how are you now in Beijing? We three have shared some happy time together. Now one by one they will leave me. Well, people have to say goodbye one day be it rainy or sunny.

April 11

It's Saturday today. All the eight girls of our dorm went to the West Willow Park. It was raining and the budding peonies dropped their heads in the heavy rain. We walked under small umbrellas and screamed hysterically in the rain. How good to be with nature! For a time I forgot about poverty, yet when muddy water sneaked into my old shoes I began to feel sad. I've registered my name with many agencies but no one seems to need a governess now. I had to hide myself again in books.

I borrowed *Latin America* this morning and spent the whole day reading, trying to forget about my cold feet and empty stomach. Then darkness came and another day was gone.

April 13

I'm so tired after the PE class. I called Yangzi. She sounded happy. So I will forget her for the moment. I have to make a living. Who can help me? I'm so hungry. Harvey can't help me. No one can help me except my family. I called my sister. She told me she dreamt of me calling her one day. I was sobbing in the phone. She got so anxious that she called me the next day. But I was out. I wanted to cry when I realized this sister who used to hate me so much in childhood actually loved me so deeply. My nephew was back from school. My sister asked him to speak to me. O, silly boy, he sounded so cute and honest. He said, "I just came back from school, auntie. Can you buy me a plane when you come back next time?" I said yes of course while something stung my eyes and tears ran down. I was relieved to know Mother was in good health. I will try to be independent but I really can't hold on any longer. I know my family is always there for me. Life is so hard. Now I begin to sympathize with Clinton who has to borrow money here and there to make a living at school. I hope I haven't hurt him.

April 14

I'm sad today. Harvey did not call me. Instead, Clinton called to tell me that his thumb was cut while he was welding some metal to earn money. I promised to see him this weekend. How I wish to take some money for him!

April 15

I got to know Mr. Zhang yesterday. He was a military doctor. He came to our classroom and asked whether somebody could help him with his English. He was going to take the national exam two months later. He would pay. There was something wrong with one of my ears and I was reading in my seat half deaf when this happened. Six was not confident to "govern" such a military man so she pulled my ponytail and urged me to have a try. I looked up to see a handsome but short man in a military uniform. I stood up and asked respectfully what the matter was. I was afraid some of my classmates were caught stealing or something. After a roar of laughter he said he needed a governess to help him with his English. Good, my heart was singing though I tried to look professional. "How much do you pay?" "Ten Yuan an hour." Ok, that was a deal. I gave him my phone number and sat down to read. Six came up to congratulate me. She winked at me with her shining black eyes and joked about a coming romance with a military man. I laughed and went back to the dorm with her. The phone rang while we were still unlocking the door. We looked at each other and smiled. It was Mr. Zhang. He invited me to dinner! I went and tried to behave like a lady while keeping an eye to any dishes that I could take home for Six. He said it was not easy to be a college student. He said, "You look so pale. You must have some nutritious food" and put some fish in my plate with his chopsticks. I was so touched by this timely care and liked him at once. Six was happy to find me back red cheeked and high spirited though I forgot to bring her the leftovers.

April 17

Evening on campus is always so inviting. I wanted to share the night with Harvey but he went out with others when I called him. I sighed and put down the phone. My roommates have gone out one by one. I was left alone in the dorm, so piteous. Then the phone rang. It was Mr. Zhang. He just called to say hello, yet that was enough to make me feel cared for and important. Thank you,

Sir.

Clinton's finger was still hurting but I did not have the money or mood to see him. I really can't waste my feelings any more.

April 18

Harvey bought me a long skirt this morning. He borrowed some money to buy me a skirt. He said it made him feel sad to see me in old clothes while other girls were catching up with the fashion. I want to cry. How can I give him up?

I miss Mr. Zhang too. He treats me like a little sister. I was trying to keep my nails long to look like an artist when he invited me to eat beef noodle one night. He was surprised at my long nails and cut them before I could resist. I felt so weird when he held my fingers in his strong hand and cut my nails within two minutes. He laughed at my fancies of being an artist and warned me that long nails contained millions of germs. How could he behave so naturally and comfortably before me while I was so nervous? I was so proud of him when he carried me on his motorbike. He looked so cool in the green uniform. I wanted to call him but did not know whether it was right or wrong.

Clinton called again this noon. I felt sorry for him. What he needs is what I can't give.

April 19

It was a miracle! My *Sands in hands* was published! I almost forgot it. While I was having supper in the dorm, a girl from the Chinese Department broke in and showed me the printed book.

I was too excited to eat anything afterwards. God, I have the ability to write! My story was put in the first place and many students who have read the book said mine was the best. Donna was as affected as me. She ran to the classroom and commanded everyone's attention to her "very important" news. It was so good to share my success with friends though I was paid nothing for the story.

April 24

I had dinner with Ryan last night. I experienced a little cultural uneasiness with him. In China it's always the boy who pays for a meal together unless the girl wants to insult the boy she won't insist to pay. So I sat there waiting for Ryan to pay. I waited and waited, and he waited too. I was not sure what the right move was. Should I follow the western way and go Dutch or should I follow the Chinese way and not insult a friend? I thought the latter choice was safer. I talked and waited and worried. Ryan seemed to be waiting, too. In the end he looked annoyed and paid. I felt very uneasy but could not talk about it openly. Then we had a walk and he asked me to buy him a bottle of *Wahaha* as if to make it up. I bought it eagerly, and laughed at his "western meanness" unconsciously.

April 26

Mr. Zhang took me to his office in a military hospital today. He tested my blood to find it was type AB. He let me share his lunch and a long cucumber. He showed me some poems by himself. I was gladly surprised to find him a quite different man under that stern military face. Then he played a beautiful song with his flute and took me back to school.

My life becomes more complicated with Zhang's appearance. I am getting more and more confused. What am I doing? Am I kissing fire? I feel bad and frightened. I can't fall in love with Mr. Zhang but I am beginning to depend on his laughter, flute and harmonica for pleasure. I wait for his call every day after lunch. He will call and sometimes we can talk for hours. What shall I do? I will sleep though I don't think it is possible. God, why do I have so many paradoxes? O, Harvey! Harvey!

May 2

Ryan is leaving today. I called him. He did not sound happy at my call at all. He said he was busy packing. He was annoyed that I should ask his address in America. I did not know why. It is just a Chinese way to do so if you are friends. So in spite of all the efforts we are not friends in the end. I threw the address he grudgingly gave to me over the phone into a dustbin. It would be an insult to me if I kept it.

May 9

I had a strange experience today. I was one of the thousands of students who marched to the street, chanted slogans and waved colorful banners in the morning. It was thrilling. We were called on to do so because the US had bombed our embassy to Yugoslav. They killed 3 Chinese journalists but did not apologize. It is a great shame and we shall not bear it. College students all over the country are showing their indignation on the streets. When the fire reached Zhengzhou yesterday, we students felt it our responsibility to stand up and do something, as the best university of this central Province Henan. Many boys threw their bowls and basins out of the window last night. This morning when we were having the intensive reading class, the dean of the department broke in. He looked worried and excited. He said all other departments were marching now. Please go downstairs quickly and join them! We put down our text books and ran down to march and to chant. The slogans we chanted were quite old and old things sometimes were provoking and touching. We waved our banners and yelled "Down with the US!" "Boycott American goods!" "Down with the capitalist!" at the top of our voice. We marched on the streets happily. Citizens came out to look at us or popped their heads out of windows to see what these monkeys were doing then slapped their windows back, seeing we were doing nothing but walking, chatting and shouting. Some citizens complained that the students had blocked their way to work. All in all, our enthusiasm met icy cynicism on the streets. So we came back to the campus after half an hour's yelling and walking. I ran up to the dorm to call Mr. Zhang. He must have something to say, being a military man. I dialed his number and was choked with emotion when his manly voice reached my thirsting ear. He comforted me by saying that you students had done right but that was enough. Go to study, girl. Leave the thing to diplomats. There is going to be no war and there shouldn't be any war. We need peace. So I came to the classroom while other students were discussing another march. I used to have such a strong aversion to politics. Not now. A crowd must have a leading group who manages things for the common good. I felt sick at the pictures of the dead Chinese journalists. How weak China still is! We have been in a weak and despised position for a long time. If a country can't stand equal with other countries, how can its people be respected. All of a sudden I want to be a diplomat. This is not a new dream. I had it in high school but gave it up gradually when I was reminded again and again that I was a woman. I was a coward. I dare not try to be a more useful woman and be what I want to be. Not now. I came back to life when shouting those hundred-year-old slogans. I want to be a diplomat! I will try my best to realize this dream. I swear.

May 11

Mr. Zhang came to see me last night. There was a debate going on in the Management Department. So we went to see what the students' opinions were. There had been lots of wall papers written in old Chinese in poetry. I was touched to see that modern students still could use the old language and tone so well. I wondered what Bill Clinton would say if he saw the intense feelings and wounded pride of these Chinese students. When the organizer of the debate asked me to give a speech, I went all emotional and promised I would translate all the wall papers into English and send them to Clinton. Zhang put cold water to our burning fire by saying that China was not in favor of war. We couldn't afford a war.

May 12

Some foreign teachers have run away to hide, not Amy and Patrick. We have such a mixed feeling towards our foreign teachers. Students of other departments called the English majors shameless spies when we were having a hard time adjusting our feelings to our American teachers. When Amy entered the classroom, we began to sing the national anthem. She cried and we cried too. She apologized to us about the death of the three Chinese journalists and said it was wrong of the US government to bomb the Yugoslav embassy. Sometimes the government did not represent the people's will. Then we began the class in a peaceful but sensitive way.

After class I went to the library to return some books. There were still many students reading and copying the poems dedicated to the US government. I rode by calmly, but on the way back I couldn't hold my tears any longer. I am a Chinese. I identify with them so easily. Their pains and bewilderments are mine too.

May 14

I have been expecting changes in my life but only good ones. When Mr. Zhang entered my life, I welcomed it as the rainbow which God gave to me after so much rainfall in my life. I did not want to refuse him until today. He seemed so kind, so promising, so knowledgeable and so mature. He was the first man who said he could read my heart. I was so relaxed and comfortable with him. Yet when he kissed me in the dark, I was terrified. I shouldn't be so open and easy- going with him. See what is happening to me! What a complicated life I am living! I can't tell Harvey about it. How I want to escape, to fly away! Harvey looks so far from me because I keep a secret in my heart. I knew clearly that I shouldn't fall in love with this half stranger Zhang. I knew so little about him. Is he married? What I long for is pure friendship not any physical touch. I can't talk to him as freely as Harvey. He changes the topic whenever I hint at it. It's a hard time for a straightforward girl like me. I hate this kind of sneaky life. It's not right and going to be dirty. Every time he touches me I urge myself to box his ears yet it is not in my nature. I am addicted to his flutes and songs when I decide to tear away from him. At least he cares about me. He gives me a sense of safety that no one has ever given and he came to me when I was most lonely and vulnerable. He has given me confidence and sunshine as well as pop corns and ice creams, hasn't he? What shall I do? God, please have mercy on me!

May 21

A new day has come. I will start a new role or continue an old one. I walk here and there, smiling wickedly. I am an actress. I don't need to worry about anything.

May 27

I went to a Chinese painting exhibition this morning. The painting class I am attending now has wakened up my fervent love in painting. I used to copy the beautiful designs on china bowls and bed sheets before I went to primary school. I had a natural tendency for beautiful things and such a strong desire to recreate them with my own hands. I walked timidly on the soft carpet of the magnificent hall, marveled at the gentle shades and expressive matches of colors of the hundreds of paintings hanging on the wall. It was fascinating to find myself in such a hall and to rub elbows with famous artists. I was so sure that if the middle school I went to could afford to give us art class I would have chosen painting as my major instead of English.

Harvey called me when I came back from the exhibition. He was sweet and tried to be good to me. I smiled without uttering a word when he asked me whether I missed him or not. He couldn't see my smile and put down the phone with a sigh.

May 30

I was furiously sad when Mr. Zhang told me he was married. He told me the truth when I questioned him about the voice of a child heard last time over the phone. He was married. He had twins and a wife! I held my breath and tears until he hung up. The man who used to sweep my heart like storm was dead now. He once walked so close to me yet was so far away from my heart now. No wonder he always looked fresh and energetic when he told me he lived a life of nightmare. He had a wife! He had a perfect family while he was flirting with me! I am feeling so dirty and so sick. God, what have I done? What shall I do?

June 1

I walked sadly to the classroom, opened my book with tears

dripping down. Life seemed so slow and heavy for me. How I wished to fly away! Away from the suffocating classroom, the lonely dormitory, the empty campus and the cruel reality! I was so tired. I went to bed early and dreamed of a temple at the foot of a mountain. I knocked at the door. It was opened by a young nun who was smiling at me. She asked me to step in. I found three more nuns weeping the floor. I saw bamboos and big flowers inside the temple. I was so happy and decided to stay with them and be a nun.

June 2

The dream last night had brought me a profound serenity. I got up early to read English in the garden, had breakfast, went to the classroom, listened to every word of the teacher's lecture and did my homework carefully. I was so at ease. I hoped someone could share my beautiful calmness. Then after lunch I called home. I told my sister I was very well and happy. Yes, I am happy. Something important is going to happen. I can feel it in the air. Something beautiful is stirring my heart.

Next Wednesday will be the last painting class. I want to give some gift to my one-armed teacher. Harvey has been with me all through the three months' painting class. He studied in the next classroom while I was painting in our room. After class he would wash my brushes and plate for me. Then he would walk me back to the dorm. Next Wednesday Harvey will wash my brush for the last time. I feel sorry about it. I feel sorry about every parting, be it a parting with the one-armed teacher or the gentle moments I shared with Harvey.

June 7

Mr. Zhang came again and left me his note book. I read it and found his heart once was so pure and noble. How I wish he hadn't changed! There was a poem he copied:

I loved you/Maybe the flame has not died out completely/ yet, let my love not bother you anymore/for I hate to see your sad eyes/I loved you and love you still/silently and gently/O, I wish other men can love you/as deeply as I do.

I always believe that even the worst man has his tender spot named love. Why do people change? They grow up and their hearts get hardened. Why did Zhang let me see his past? Did I remind him of something lost? I shall not walk too far. Don't touch me anymore, Zhang. If you ever cared about me, let us be true to each other and let our spirits speak in everlasting words. Leave me alone to Harvey for I have no love for you. What I do have for you is sympathy and friendship. I can't help telling Harvey I love him when he embraces me warmly and kisses me in a way as if there was no tomorrow. I permitted guilty tears to wet his new shirt.

June 12

I feel bad today. Nothing is interesting any longer. I am poor and helpless. I need the first scholarship. Can I get it? No, I am too creative for that. I see it as an insult to my brain to remember so many theories and given answers. What shall I do? Blow my harmonica in the fresh air! *Two tigers, two tigers, running fast! One without a tail and the other lost one ear. So strange! So strange!* I blew this simple song and laughed at the picture flashing in my mind's eye. I cheered myself up and went back to the dorm for lunch. Alas, there was only 14 Yuan left in my dining card! I was thrown to the bottom of poverty again. I have waited for some miracle, but miracles never come. No rich prince will come my rescue. I have to walk my hard way step by step. I must make some changes. What shall I do this afternoon? I don't want to bother anyone including Harvey who is a muddy Buddha in the water himself. I feel so puzzled.

June 14

So many things ---good and bad, happy and sad---crowded into June the 13th. I don't know what will happen next but I have to get on with my business. Love is still unseen. I can't forgive Harvey's past. I can't help feeling cheated whenever I remembered his diaries about another girl. I am alone now. Thank God, I am free at last. I don't know how long I have to strive and suffer before an angel would come to pull me up into a peaceful and pure paradise.

O, it is so wonderful to forgive! I can't help calling Zhang's number. He sounded as cheerful as usual, not affected by my coldness at all. If I am addicted to his voice, I have to quit this bad habit little by little. I can't think too much now. I know it's dangerous to let loose my wild imagination, but don't people quit smoking gradually? I'm in a good mood now. I can forgive anyone even Harvey. I am a saint now. I called Harvey and apologized for my bad behavior last night with laughter. I can tolerate everything now. Let him marry the girl in his diary and I would write them a poem in praise of their marriage! Am I awake or asleep? My pulse of life is beating very strongly now. I feel so right. Harvey is good, Zhang is good and I am good too. I needn't scold myself for anything. Well, I think it is all right to keep in touch with Zhang if I don't get too close to him. I am not a little girl any more. A floor full of cigarette ends does not send a thrill to me any more. Men can cry their eyes out for me but I just refuse to be moved. The summer is coming. My blood gets warmer and warmer, my spirit higher and higher. I am ready to enjoy life and be an actress again.

June 15

I dreamt of something exciting last night. Several foreign students came to study in China. I said "hi!" to them and we became friends. I asked a girl with long and golden hair where she came from and she answered me in Chinese "ZhiLi". Immediately I thought of Chile. The youngest girl seemed only 4 years old or so. I liked her very much. We went to attend a lecture. Then I promised to show them some azalea which I had never seen in real life. I was so worried about where to find azalea when a saint came up to tell me that "the past is but a beautiful memory". I felt relieved at his comforting words and turned up to see him. Yet he was gone. I woke up to tell my roommates about this strange dream. We all wondered why I dreamt of azalea which was a kind of sad and mysterious flower in Chinese culture. Maybe I am destined to become an azalea next life?

It's raining now. I feel relaxed and want to get wet in the rain. It's raining heavier now. I hope farmers have already got the ripen wheat in. Zhang once told me that he always felt depressed on rainy days. I wonder what he is doing now. I remember my first night with Harvey in the park. It was raining so hard the next morning. We had to wait in front of a bank for the rain to stop. It did not stop so we ran in the heavy rain. He looked very gloomy that rainy morning. Now, I've been worried and sad since I neglected Harvey for Zhang's sake. Rain, rain, please wash away my sorrows and guilt. The gentle wind sends the fragrance of the earth through my open window with several rain drops. I take a deep breath of the earthly scent and get drunk. The grey sky brings me a deep, wild, ancient and remote sensation. I love rain as if I can also let out some hidden sorrows with the crying of Heaven. I open my arms to welcome the rain, the pouring tears and the dripping angels.

June 16

It's funny to realize that everything is as usual when you get up in the morning. Wednesday is still a common day. The water is still running and I am still writing in the classroom. The sky is definitely blue after the rain. Green leaves are glistering in the sunshine. The spire of the nearby TV station grows straight into the pure white cloud. A flock of birds disappear behind a tall building. The old city clock beat 9 times neatly after a slow and nostalgic song of Chairman Mao. I am recovering from a kind of deadly wound now. I am calm and quiet.

God, what an evening! Zhang searched the library to look for me and then followed me to the classroom. What is the good of coming here to see me, Zhang, when you are not my perfect model anymore? I felt so disappointed when he laughed in my face and called me a silly girl who knew nothing about politics. The government was calling on military men to fight the Yangtze flood which had brought so many deaths in southern China. I encouraged Zhang to go. Many troops were there putting sand bags in the furious river and helping the desperate farmers. I saw President Jiang Zemin on the TV. He was boosting the soldiers' spirit by directing the rescue in the rain. If it was really political propaganda, so what, he was doing something. What have you done, Zhang? What right do you have to laugh at the brave ones when you are a coward yourself? Zhang's image collapsed in my heart in spite of his elegant uniform. He can't be the beacon light that can lead me to a pure and meaningful life. He looks at the world with his cynical eyes and discourages me to be healthy and trusting. Goodbye Zhang, I am so over with you.

June 19

Yesterday was Double Fifth's Day, a Chinese day to remember the dead. It was a crazy day for me. I lived it in a dream with a gallant knight on the grassland by the bank of the Golden River. O, God, did you send this man to me? Why is he exactly the one that often comes up in my dream? I was astonished when he walked up to me at the north gate of Zhengzhou University.

Was he a real man? Why did he look so familiar to me? His shining black eyes with a dash of sadness, his Chairman Mao's hair style, his high nose and perfect lips----all these have appeared in my dreams since long time ago. I gazed at him as if he was too perfect to be real. He looked a little bit shy. He bought me a bottle of green tea and we went to have a walk by the bank. I asked him whether I knew him. He laughed and said maybe. He looked so happy to be with me. He smiled a lot and talked in a tender voice. Then his mobile rang. Somebody had prepared a banquet for him. He would go but he lingered. He held my hand so naturally half an hour after we saw each other. I was drunk with his manly beauty. He drew me close and kissed me. Alas, what a kiss! I was electrified. My dreamy prince kissed me! I ceased to exist in this world anymore. I was so lifted up by a magical power. A profound sense of loss wrapped me when he left me for his banquet. He whispered he would come to me soon and asked me to wait for him. I said yes. He insisted that I promise to wait for him. I said yes again for I couldn't talk much. I was not Patricia any more. I was a silly doll dancing to his magical wand. I would do whatever it took to please him. He left me for the banquet while I went to the dorm and lay down on my wooden bed. He called me half an hour later. He said he must see me. He couldn't eat anything. He missed me too much. So I put on the long skirt Harvey bought for me and ran down stairs to see my prince. It was totally dark but I could feel his existence. I could reach for him with closed eyes. His charming eyes were like the song of sirens, pulling me to him. He put his arm around my waist and kissed me. We sat on the grassland, gazing at each other. Then we fell down in the grass. I hummed unconsciously and fell asleep. We were wakened up by the early birds who were singing in the tree above us. He smiled a mischievous smile and pulled some grass from my hair. We had breakfast together and then he had to leave for another city. He lingered so that I could say some sweet words but I said nothing. What else could I expect? I didn't even want to know his name, his address or his job. He was the biggest truth. Thank almighty God, he really existed. I walked quickly back to the campus while he entered a taxi. I couldn't look back. I couldn't believe he left me by taxi. He should fly above the crowd and melt with the rising sun. I went to lie down on my small bed. God, what happened? Was it a dream? Did we make love last night? I fell asleep, woke up in the late afternoon and declared to my roommates that I was changed. The Patricia they knew was no more. I was a different person now.

June 20

Something is even too heavy for a diary to carry. So I have to hold it with my heart and my heart sinks when it gets heavier and heavier. My God, what am I going to do? Several birds are flying in the grey and quiet sky, taking away my heart and soul. Is the magical prince Lin missing me? Why am I so sad?

June 21

Another of my prose has been published in the school newspaper. Some readers have kept asking me what I was trying to say in it. I really don't know. Maybe words are beautiful enough for their existence.

Lin is on my mind day and night. The feeling is too strong to express in words and too beautiful to share with anyone else. It is the first time in my life that I have a secret all to myself. It's the source of my invisible sorrow, puzzle and happiness.

June 22

I was dragged into real life by Harvey's poverty. I went to an agency with him and urged him to register his name for a tutor job. He was excited as if he were a millionaire already and bought me a nice cake. Poor boy!

Lin called me last night and now I am quite sure that I was not dreaming on Double Fifth's Day. His call paved a cheerful day for me.

Mr. Zhang came last night and said I was proud. Well, yes I am. I am proud of a beautiful love. Yet when I thought of my families I had to calm down. So I devoted the whole night reading English and doing homework, forgetting Zhang's coughs and sighs completely. Harvey is too young and too simple to notice any change in me. I hope I am on the right track to a meaningful and useful life. I would think of Lin after a period of fervent study. He was so tender. I decide never to say a harsh word to him. I also hope both of us can be sensible enough to cultivate this unearthly infatuation into love. I don't know what I am holding fast to is a dream or not but I am so happy about it. Be kind to me, Lin. It's raining now. Your princely eyes are smiling in the rain. You asked me whether I missed you or not last night. How can I not miss you!

June 24

Lin called. I picked up the receiver at the first ring. He said he was disappointed when I hadn't called him for such a long time. He said he was responsible for what he said and did that night. He was talking in a loud voice which upset me a little. Angels don't speak loud. Maybe my dreamy prince has come down to earth for my sake. He said I was the loveliest girl he had ever met though I did not have a pretty face. Well, should I be happy or annoyed? I hope I am encouraged to keep our relationship on a noble and interesting path. I've been looking for an aim to strive for. Now Lin is ahead of me. He is my strength.

Lin called again just now. He asked me whether I would go to see his parents with him. I did not know how to answer. This was all too fast. I'm really a little confused now. He came to the real world too soon for my swirling head. He said I was around him every moment. I want to be serious about him but, well, something is wrong.

June 25

Lin called twice last night. He was a little bit drunk. He said he kept thinking of that night. He couldn't concentrate on his job. He had lost interest in other friends. I felt good at his confession and went to bed happily. As soon as I lay down, the phone rang again. It was Lin, a mad Lin; he said life was so unbearable without me. He said he liked me very much and hoped that we could continue this relationship. He was so forceful and emotional that I did not know what to say to make him believe that I was as deep in love as he was. He said what he loved in me was not my appearance but my character. He thought I would be helpful to his career. I didn't know how to respond to this point. I hope there are two lives blooming as we really walk together in life instead of one blooming while the other withered. I asked Six about this idea. She sighed, "Love you, love you all." Jane Austen said: a girl's imagination runs fast. It jumps from admiration to love, from love to marriage within a moment. I am practicing her philosophy now.

I called Lin this noon and found Shanghai was raining. I cursed myself for not reminding him to put on more clothes. How can I express my care for him? May God bless you, my prince Lin.

Six told me very seriously that she liked my wildness. She felt depressed whenever I was lost in my thought but happy when I danced in my childish delight. I am an extreme girl. I can be the happiest girl and love the world to my bones.

June 26

I called Lin. He sounded as pleasant as a good boy. He was on the bike of his friend to whom he was telling something about me. I wished I could cry out my longings for him but tears did not come easily when I was happy.

June 27

I have spent the whole afternoon in the dorm painting some flowers for No.1. Today is her birthday. I am too poor to buy her any gift but true enough to feel happy for her.

Lin hasn't called yet. I am as quiet as the moon now though I can be as wild as wind the next minute.

June 28

Lin called twice this noon. He begged me to write a letter to him. I did so just now. It was wonderful to make my thoughts known to him. I am penniless now. I have to borrow ten Yuan from Six to post the letter.

June 29

The moon is so beautiful tonight, bright and gentle. There is not a suitable person to appreciate this with me.

Lin called three times today but I received none. I called back and he chatted as happily as usual while I was sad and annoyed. How can Cinderella share the prince's pleasure when she is dying of poverty? I did not say a sweet word to Lin who never asked my situation. He said he would come to see me if he had time. I said calmly that if he did not have time he need not come to see me. He was surprised at my response and denied it. Gosh, I was out of my mind. I said goodbye coldly and hung up. He called again and said in a wounded tone that he would be upset if I continued in this impersonal way. I said I did it deliberately. I was sad. I couldn't wait see him when I needed him so much. He coaxed me and promised to come as soon as possible. I found comfort and safety in the way he spoke and put down the phone gently. It rang again. This time it was Harvey. He felt so bad these days that I was afraid to talk to him. God, please forgive me.

I sigh so heavily as if there is an elephant on my chest. I don't know which one to choose. Actually I know but I can't make the decision.

July 1

I don't know whether Lin will call or not. What shall I say to him if he really calls? He is on my mind as naturally as the sun and the moon are. Yet I feel so silly and humble on hearing his expressive and powerful voice. He is the happy prince shining in the sun while I am the poor match girl dreaming of roasted duck and a pair of warm shoes. I wonder what he likes in me; surely not my trouble nor my hot temper. He is so gentle sometimes. It makes me feel ashamed to be angry with him.

Chapter Eight

The only Summer

July 3

Summer vacation has started. The girl's dormitory building needs to be repaired. So we have to move all our things to classrooms. It is a great chance for boys. They have a full breakfast and come to the Building No 8 on bikes or with wheel carts. Harvey is one of them. He is in good mood now that he can see me the whole day. He helps me packing bags and bags of old shoes and small articles, takes all the bags and cases downstairs, puts them on a wheel cart, rides the cart to the classroom building and lifts all the bags and cases to the fifth floor. I see sweat coming down his face. He is really a qualified worker. Thank you, dear Harvey. We are the same. I just can't imagine Lin doing all these manual works. No, my angel is destined to fly and dance. He would cease to exist if I drag him to earth and let him see my shabby clothes and dirty shoes.

I won't go home for this vacation. I need to find a job and earn some money. What's more, I need to wait for Lin who has promised me to come to Zhengzhou. Zhang has found a room for Eva and me. Thank you, man. I remind myself to keep a distance from him.

Clinton asked me out tonight. He recited me a love poem and asked me to be his girlfriend. He was enraged and changed to another frightening person when I told him I had Harvey as my boyfriend. He almost pushed me down the river. Silly man. Pooh, I laughed coldly at his disgusting behavior and went back to the dorm.

Lin called just now and said he had received my letter today and had read it several times. Will he abandon me when he finds out that I am a poor girl from the countryside? Will he despise me because that pair of crystal shoes have changed into a pumpkin? Can he understand my feelings for Harvey? What will happen? Maybe I shouldn't be so honest. I give myself totally up and wait impatiently for a verdict.

July 4

I moved into the flat which Zhang found for me and Eva. It was located in the residential area of the Armed Police of Zhengzhou. So, literally we would live with the families of military men this summer. Eva decided to rebel against her traditional and protective family and had a taste of independence.

It was a small but nice room with TV and cooking utensils but no telephone. I had to run downstairs to call Lin. He did not answer me.

My student, Little Ox's mother gave me 200 Yuan as my pay

for the whole summer vacation. It was very kind of her to pay me first so that I could settle down quickly.

July 5

We got up at exactly 6 am when the broadcast started blowing its penetrating horns. It was still raining. Eva went out to look for a job while I sat in the tiny room, thinking of Lin. After remote yet strong horns there came slow and gentle music from the broadcast. My heart was filled in with inexpressible emotions in the early morning. How I wish to share this healthy and fresh life with Lin! I had the whole room to myself and felt lonely. I didn't want to move as if my arms were tied up by time. I felt so useless. Why was I here? For Lin! Yet I was afraid of calling him. I still can't tell dream from reality. I am free and lonely.

I called Lin this afternoon. He said he would fly to Zhengzhou the day after tomorrow. Ah, is it real? My heart is dancing and singing at such good news. I pray nothing would ever change his care for me.

I must do something to keep this beautiful love. It is the strength of my life.

July 6

It's still raining very hard. Lin would be cold when he comes here. I'll call to tell him to wear more clothes. I had my hair dyed black last night. I want to look good. I had never cared so much about my appearance until I knew Lin. Lin, please come quickly. I miss you so much though I am afraid of seeing you. I've almost forgotten your appearance. O, come to me quickly!

Zhang came to see me this afternoon. I wish so much that he were Lin so that I could lean against his shoulder and tell him how I miss him. Yet Zhang was not Lin so my heart wept when it found being cheated. Lin, please come to me!

July 8

Lin came to see me yesterday. He hugged me so tightly and desperately that we became one within a second. We went to have a walk by the bank, holding hands. So content was I! I would die with him as happily as a lark. We walked and kissed and hugged. I was transfixed again under his magical wand. We went to lie down in the grassland. He was tired after the long journey and fell asleep. I sat in the moonlight and drank in his beauty greedily. His dark and elegant eyebrows, his long and trembling lashes, his juicy lips---why was he so beautiful? I sat there chasing mosquitoes for my prince and covered him with my shirt when it was getting cold in the early morning. He was my baby. I was willing to do anything for him. When the first ray shone on the horizon I bent down and kissed him. He opened his eyes and murmured, "Marry me." I smiled but said nothing for I was still wondering whether he was a real man or not. The sun would rise and he would disappear, and I would be left with the reality and the loneliness.

July 9

My bike was confiscated by the police when I did not stop for the red light. I walked two hours to teach a student and came back to wait for Lin. I waited and waited but he did not come. I painted three paintings and sang to myself.

July 10

I lost my bike yesterday. The traffic police took it away in a truck. I walked here and there but could not have it back. They told me it was stolen. Farewell, my green bike. I don't know what will happen to you. I hope Lin can help me buy a new bike. I hate to ask him for help but who else can I turn to. Harvey has gone home. Zhang is here but I won't bother him anymore. It is so embarrassing to ask Lin for help. I am tired. I want to go home. Tears are running down my face.

Life makes us hard and cool. When Eva lost her new beeper I did not try to comfort her. I knew it was helpless. I can't share my feelings with her when I am so emotional, sensitive, confused, sad and puzzled. We share one bed but do not communicate effectively. We are lost in our respective worries and thoughts. While Eva is struggling to make a living all by herself, I am thinking of Lin. How can I enter his heart? How can I understand him? He asked me whether it was right for him to love me and I answered "yes" without hesitation. Do you love me, Lin? Then why can't you see my knotted brows and tearful eyes? I bought a bottle of beer. It was so bitter but I washed it down my throat. Lin told me maybe he would leave for Xi'an this afternoon. Who am I? Nobody! I am just a toy for him. No, never! Why not be kind to me since you love me? You, a hypocrite! Tears brushed my cheeks gently while I was drinking. I want to escape. I hope to lose all my senses and wake up to find a world full of sunshine, flowers and birds. Well, I am still sober now though my head is getting heavy. I should have gone to teach another student if I am not waiting for Lin. He said he would come to see me after this and that. Oh, I hate to be treated as an extra person. Ok, I will wait. If he does not come, it is not my fault to give up this damned fantasy. If he does not come this afternoon, I shall begin a new life bravely. If he comes, he must give me a definite sense of security.

Ah, someone was knocking at the door! I ran to open it and find my handsome prince. However, he looked so cold. He walked in, sat on the chair and declared that he came here to part with me forever. He said I was a bad girl and did not know what love was. I was trembling all over while he bent down to write something on the desk. I was so frightened. What should I do if I lose him? What should I do if I lose my own life? I couldn't find answers to my questions and burst into tears. I sat on the bed sobbing while he left me and closed the door behind him. My prince deserted me! Because I was a girl without principle! Because I love him too much! I collapsed in the bed and cried. Then the door was open. Lin entered in with mischief in his laughing eyes. He held me in his arms and wiped my tears with his lips. He said he was playing a joke on me to see whether I loved him or not. Alas, what a joke! He patted my cheeks gently and said I was a silly little girl. He stood up, drew on the curtain and put me gently on the bed. We moved slowly into each other. Then he left me in the setting sun. I stood on the balcony and saw he turned back and waved his hand.

I returned to the room and pressed his photo to my heart.

July 11

Little Ox's family invited me to go bowling yesterday. It was my first time to play this expensive game and I felt quite self-conscious among the rich- looking people. After the game we went to have McDonald's. I believe it was quite expensive too, for Little Ox's parents went out to eat pancakes at a small stand after ordering some hamburger and fried chicken for me. I was so touched. They are such a nice couple. I have made up my mind to improve Little Ox's English quickly and efficiently.

I called Lin just now to find everything was Ok. I am so afraid of losing him. No, this is not the right mentality. I must be confident. I will look for another job tomorrow. I will stay in Zhengzhou as long as possible so that when Lin comes again on a business trip he can see me.

July 13

Harvey came to Zhengzhou. He was so excited to see me after more than a week's absence. I told him everything about Lin and cried hysterically for my piteous Harvey. He was as kind as usual and gentler. I cried and cried till both of us believed that I would die from shedding too many tears. I don't know whether it is right or wrong to choose Lin. Why am I so sad if I have made the right choice? Harvey wiped my tears and combed my hair silently. What have I done? If Lin tells me he does not care for me at all, I would stop missing him. Yet he has said again and again that he loved me. I am not hankering after vanity but love. May God punish me if I were wrong!

Eva is not happy tonight. I can see her frowned eyebrows in the moon light. I'm sorry Eva. Patricia is too sad to comfort you. May some angels bring good messages in your dream!

July 14

I found another governess job yesterday. Harvey has never said a harsh word about my story with Lin. He puts me high above himself. If I am sad he would be sad. If I cry for Lin's coming and Harvey would pray that Lin should come quickly. Compared with Clinton, who almost pushed me into the river, Harvey is a real sage. I can never leave him from the bottom of my heart.

July 15

Gazing at Lin's handsome photo is sweeter than eating an ice cream after I come back from teaching. I hope he is tender and true to me as I to him.

July 16

Eva has gone to teach. I am left alone in the room and feel lonely without someone to speak to. I sit by the window, watching children running happily on the playground. I dreamt of my poor eldest sister last night. She is the sister who had insisted that I should be sent to the hospital when I was dying from a high fever. My foolish father was urging everyone in the family to work in the field. His dear garlic sprouts were getting old every day. I was not even as dear as garlic to him. Children were like weed in the countryside. They grow or die. Mother told me that I was purple all over after three days of high fever. She combed my hair while I lay unconscious in bed. She could not bear to see me dead with a head of lice. My eldest sister wouldn't let me go. She held my cold hand crying and insisted that I be sent to the hospital quickly. Mother was touched and borrowed a wheel cart and took me to a hospital where I was saved. My eldest sister has never mentioned this part to me. She still cursed me when I followed her everywhere, dragging a corner of her shirt. Yet she would save some delicacies for me when I went to middle school in town. She would count the days of my coming home and cook my favorite dish for me. Then she would carry my bundle of washed clothes and canned prickles and saw me off to school again. She would ask the driver to promise that he would take me to the gate of my school.

I am a grown-up now, making dreams and love in a big city while my eldest sister has been married to a poor farmer and is living a wretched life. How many times have I woken with a wet pillow worrying about my poor sister!

July 17

Harvey invited me to have an outing with him yesterday afternoon. I was like a bird out of the metal cage. I jumped and screamed on the vast grassland. Harvey was happy because I was happy. I took his hand and let him run wildly with me. But how could I forget my princely Lin? I called him while Harvey was cooking dinner for us. Lin was ill. He sounded weak and tired. I was startled. Lin was never like this. He was as energetic as a tiger. What was wrong? Maybe I shouldn't have hung out with Harvey. Was there a cosmic effect? Had Lin sensed my happiness in the wild with Harvey? I was too upset to eat the noodle which Harvey had made spicy to cater for my flavor.

July 18

Harvey was in need of a job badly otherwise he would have to go home. We went out in the early morning to look for a job for him. We asked restaurants and shops whether they need a waiter. No, they didn't need any new man to share their small pie. We walked around the city but could not find a job for him. To boost our spirits we bought a bottle of mineral water and went to have a rest in a park. We shared the water and hugged and cried. Suddenly a head popped out of the woods behind us. I was so surprised to find Clinton wandering ghostly in the woods. He looked steadily into my eyes and said he sensed my coming so he was waiting for me. I introduced him to Harvey. They shook hands like good comrades. Clinton took out some apples from his pocket. He said they were from our hometown and especially for me. I accepted the apples and shared them with Harvey when Clinton disappeared in the dark woods.

July 19

It is terribly hot these days. Little Ox's parents invited me to go swimming with them. His mother, Ms. Li, was a very kind person. She taught me how to hold my breath under water and also let me use a lot of her shampoo. How lovely to see people under water! I held my breath; half opened my eyes and marveled at so many legs and bottoms in the water. We stayed in the water till very dark to make the fullest use of the tickets and then went to have some seafood—another first in my life. I thanked them in my heart and wished to help Little Ox improve his English with all my tricks. I was thinking of Lin all the time. I miss him so much and hope he misses me more.

July 20

I was in the room alone. It was stuffy and hot. I wanted to go swimming again but couldn't afford it. "Bang, bang, bang" somebody was knocking at the door. I opened it. Gosh, a group was coming--- Six and her boyfriend Dragon, and Eva who had just came back from teaching, and my Harvey. I cooked some noodle for the dear troop. After lunch we each found a place to have a nap. Six, Dragon and Eva squeezed in the wooded bed, Harvey fell asleep on the floor and I sat in my chair, gazing at Lin's photo. I miss him too much which is not good for my mind. Life should be easy and wonderful for everyone. However, Harvey is very depressed these days, especially today. He kissed me almost to screaming point. I know he is suffering a lot, yet his character determines that he won't quarrel with me nor hate me for leaving him at the very moment when he is getting serious with me. I'm sorry, Harvey. God, bless my boy. Six's left cheek ha swollen. May God bless her, too. We went swimming after they woke up from the nap. Then we had dinner together. Zhang came with his twins when we were out. I had missed the chance to see his darlings. It is very kind of him to care for me when I have given my heart to Lin. I have almost lost three of my boy friends for Lin. Harvey is sad; Clinton is mad; Zhang is disappointed. What about Lin? Maybe he is glad. He left me for Xi'an ten days ago. It was like ten years. I tried not to call him and slapped my hand when I really called him.

Where are you, Lin? My happiness has been soaked with tears since you left me. I've determined again and again not to miss you, but, there is a feeling creeping in my vein and stirring my longing for you. Come, please. One hour would be enough. Fold me in your arms and let me feel your love.

Six came to see me at noon. How I wish she were you!

July 24

I posted Lin a letter this morning. I won't call him till he receives the letter. It's very important to let him know my feelings. God please help me to find an everlasting love this time. I've refused all the other boys for Lin. I hope for a good ending to my sad and colorful life though I am not good from time to time.

July 25

Why are there so many beggars in the city? Some look very strong and healthy. Why don't they work? I went to find answers to my questions in the railway station. It was hot. I bent down to ask a woman beggar who was crawling on the dirty ground,

"Granny, why are you a beggar?" She did not reply. I thought she was dying from the heat. So I bought a bottle of water and put it in front of her. She looked up and squeezed a faint smile at me. I asked her again, "Why do you beg in the hot sun? Do you have children?""Yes, I have three sons. They are starving too." I asked her why she didn't work. It was more decent to earn her bread by being a cleaner. She sat up and sighed. Yes, she was quite willing to be a cleaner but laid-off city people had already grabbed all the chances. She had no choice but crawling on the ground to beg. I thought of myself and many of my friends when she was talking. It was not that we were lazy. There are just too many people but too few jobs. I was discouraged from the investigation. What is the use of knowing the cry of the poor? We can all see it and we are all suffering it as a nation. I can do nothing about it at this moment. So I gave up being a journalist and came back to my room. At least I have a shelter in this hot and crowded city.

July 27

I dreamt of the days when my sisters were still not married. I dreamt and dreamt till I was too tired to say goodbye to Eva when she went out to teach. Am I missing my family? My little niece was so happy to see me. She ran to me while yelling, "My auntie is home!" O, how I want to see her! How I need a child to share my lonely days with! How I want to buy some small gifts for them! Suddenly I realized that I still have so much besides men's love. Yes, I can be happy at home

August 6

Lin will come to Zhengzhou today on a "business trip". I need to be with him.

My new bike is confiscated again. I was reading in the book store and came out to find my new bike gone. Some people said they saw it was thrown onto a truck driven by traffic police. Maybe my bike was put beyond the white line drawn for the "beautification of our city". Shit! Why didn't they notify me? They are no better than thieves! I am outraged. Alas, what can I do in this policemen "wholeheartedly-served" country! I have to go to beg them, and give them money and if my bike is still not sold they may give it back to me. My poor two-week-old bike, what will happen to you?

August 7

My bike is gone. I walked to all the police stations but could not find it. I walked here and there in misguided directions and smiled gently to our dear policemen one station after another. Sometimes they shouted at me. Sometimes they showed me all the confiscated bikes, hundreds of them. When I told them my bike was a new one they laughed and said you'd better go home. New bikes were easily sold. I walked miles and miles with Eva. She felt for my loss of the new bike while I felt for her poor feet and dry lips. So I bought a water melon and shared with her under a big tree on the dirty street. Money was too precious to buy tickets so after the watermelon we walked five more miles and got home in the dark.

Zhang was waiting for us at the playground with his twins. We invited them upstairs and I ran down to buy the kids two small watermelons. We were eating and playing with the kids when somebody knocked at the door. It was Lin. My handsome prince stood there with a huge watermelon over his shoulder. Zhang was so annoyed at this beautiful guest that he hastened away with his twins who were quite happy to stay with the watermelons. He spanked their little asses and dragged them away. Lin was amused. He couldn't understand why this military man was annoyed at his coming. His big black eyes were laughing when Zhang banged the door behind him. Then he invited me and Eva to take a bath in his hotel room. Taking a bath in his room? I was surprised at such an idea and Eva was terrified. What did he mean by taking a bath in his room? He looked at us and laughed. He said, "You two look so tired and dirty after a day's walk. What's wrong with a hot bath free of charge?" He just couldn't believe we walked the whole city to look for the bike. He laughed at our stupidity and gave me 200 Yuan to buy a new bike. Then we walked to his hotel through the park where I had my first night with Harvey. Harvey? His sad eyes flashed in my mind. He had gone home a week ago. I was too happy to feel guilty then. We walked to his hotel and each had a bath. Then he sent us off in a taxi. So nothing was wrong with a bath in a man's room. Eva was as happy as a little angel. She said Lin was the most handsome and gentle man she had ever seen. It was purely good luck to just behold such a man. Well, just think, I, Patricia, have him!

August 23

I came back home yesterday to find the economic condition worse than ever. I can't tell my parents I have earned nothing for a month's work in Zhengzhou. It's hard for me to ask them for the 4,000 Yuan tuition. What shall I do? I think of Lin. May I ask him for help? What will happen if I ask him to lend me some money? To be frank I am not very confident of his love for me. God, please be merciful. I need money as well as love. I hope Lin can understand my situation.

August 24

I went to see my sister-in-law who was still hiding in the fields. She did not agree that I should ask Lin for money. But who else can I turn to? My brother is trying so hard to keep all his children out of hunger. I just can't bear to burden him anymore. His guilty and piteous eyes are enough to kill my heart.

I do hope Lin can understand me. If one day I marry him, it is not for money but love.

God, please help your child!

August 26

With one hand pressing my fast beating heart, I called Lin's number. Sorry, he couldn't help me. He had just repaired his broken tooth which cost him 400 Yuan. I said ok, hung up and hid my burning and tearful face in my bed sheet. O, I hate him! I hate him! He sounded so cold when I needed so much courage to ask him for help. I looked at his photo and made up my mind to burn it.

At last it was my second sister who helped me. I went to town to borrow money from Rong one of my best friends in middle school. She just got engaged and agreed to lend me 500 Yuan out of her 2,000 Yuan dowry gift. When we were withdrawing the 500 Yuan from a bank my sister came. I was embarrassed to death, letting my sister see me borrowing money. She smiled at Rong, thanked her and put 2,000 Yuan in my hand. Something stung my nose. I tried not to cry in front of them. I did not even thank them. I said goodbye causally and took the bus home.

Chapter Nine

Last Hug before His Disappearance

August 28

I am in dorm room 202 now. I am not happy. I left home with depression and came back with no friends to welcome me.

August 30

I had a heart-broken dream this noon. My neighbor betrayed me, my mother was lost and I was left in the darkness alone at home. I called Lin twice after the disturbing nap. He didn't answer the phone. Has he forgotten me? Have all my friends forgotten me? How cruel they are!

September 2

I cried on my birthday. The two boys whom I loved most haven't called to say "Happy Birthday". It's not that their empty words could really make me happy. How heartless my friends are! Let the day pass quickly. I'll go on. I'll study. My friends, please regret when you remember the love I have given to you.

I think of Yangzi. How is she now? Has that American Donald written to her? I doubt it.

September 3

I smile to my roommates as happily as usually but my heart is crying. I still can't believe I have been played like a fool. I have called Lin again and again but he just did not answer it. God damn you, bad boy! How can I believe you are a cheater when your eyes shine so innocently?

September 6

I posted a long letter to Lin today.

I've caught a cold. I kept sneezing at class and came back to the dorm when I used up the tissues. I hope Lin is fine.

September 16

Lin came to Zhengzhou the day before yesterday. We spent a sweet night together in a room rented by his client. I bought a new jacket in the morning and in the evening I was tightly in his arms. He pressed me all over his attractive body and we were a happy one in that hard wooden bed. How I relaxed in his arms! He closed his beautiful eyes and said Zhengzhou was sweeter than his home. He had been thinking of me every day and missed me as much as I missed him. He was sorry about not helping me with my tuition. He was in a little trouble. He looked into my searching eyes and said seriously, "Believe me little girl, I am working for us. I want to earn lots of money for you. Whenever I am tired I would think of you and I would strive on. Business is hard now but I won't give up trying."I was too embarrassed to touch on this point. So I murmured, "I am hungry!" He got up and boiled four eggs. I finished my two eggs quickly and looked at him. He patted my head like a big brother and shared the last egg with me. I was so so so happy! We went to bed again and locked in each other's arms. He told me his hard past while some tender music floating in the air. He was the only boy in his family and he mother spoiled him. But he ran away to earn big money after a fight with his father. His mother followed him with his ID card and cried. He wouldn't go home no matter how his mother begged him. Thus he started his way in the world with an ID card and an old camera. He tried a lot of things. He used to work in a construction group and slept in the fields. Then he went to Ningbo, a commercial city in southeast China and worked as a salesman in a big Taiwanese-owned company. He was still working in the company where he was quite an important person now. I kissed his hand gently at the part when he slept in the field with mosquitoes and rats. No matter how poor he was or had been, he was my prince. I was content to live in a hut with his love. The moon had come up and shone on our bed. He whispered to me, "Honey, will you marry me?" I thought he was joking so I did not answer but fell asleep. He woke me up the next morning and urged me to go back to school. He said, "Study hard, girl" and stopped a taxi for me. I was right on time for Amy's listening class. I sat among my classmates, so calm and relaxed. Six winked at me knowingly. I smiled at her. How I wanted to kiss every one of my friends and share my happiness with the world!

October 28

Three months have passed in the new semester. The autumn is here with gentle breeze and golden leaves. I read *Sister Carrie* in the garden and see myself in her through my misty eyes. I am too poor to think about love and marriage now. I look down at my shabby clothes then at the crispy fallen leaves and suddenly feel very old. I've never been a girl. I have been an old woman since I was born in 1978. My hands and feet are still fat and fresh, but look into my eyes you will see so much sorrow and loneliness. How I wish to have a husband like Hexi who took care of Echo in the Sahara Desert! I am scared when I think of the life Carrie lives in the end. She is not able to love any more. She is dead inside. Will I become another Carrie? No. Maybe my depression is brought by the special atmosphere of the autumn. This season is like an elegy for the death of youth when it reaches the peak of its glory. A profound helplessness devours my heart when I look up at the vast grey sky and down at the dead leaves. No one can hold the exuberant summer back. No one can hold his youth back. I closed the book and was transfixed to a Carrie in a moment. I'm even tired of Lin. Who is he? Where is he? No big deal. All will be gone like the fallen leaves. I am tired of it all.

November 27

Harvey walked slowly by the bank when I asked to end the relationship with him. I couldn't bear to see his swollen eyes and tear-stricken face. So I ran to the dorm and looked at my piteous boy through the window. How lonely he was! He did not say a word when I said goodbye to him defiantly. When I watched him through the window suddenly I saw a heart bleeding. He was so like me. He was a part of me! How could I tear myself apart and that half of me drifting among the swirling leaves! I stood by the window crying aloud till my roommates forced me to lie on bed.

November 30

I am a rebel now. I do not talk much. I would walk quickly to the library while my roommates are still gossiping about boys and teachers. I pick up the old green bag which reminds people of Chairman Mao's Long March, put on my broken shoes and run to the library. I sit at wherever I like, neglecting all the books and notes that are put on the table to say that the owner would come in ten minutes. I am a philosopher and philosophers should have their own style! My silent Long March style attracts a boy named Vinegar. He came up to me one day and asked me a grammar question. I gave him an answer and bent down over my books again. After a while he pushed my elbow and showed me a grammar book. He said my answer was wrong according to the book. I looked up at him and said clearly, "Don't worry about the book. I am always right." He stared at me with a thumb in his mouth till I laughed through my nose and reminded him that only idiots would stare at people in that way. He said he was my fan and asked my phone number. The next day he found me in the library and showed me his Long March style bag. He said I looked so cool with that washed bag that he bought one himself. I began to like this silly boy. Yesterday morning when I was reading on the grassland by the bank, Vinegar came with his cool bag. He sat beside me and took out an apple. He peeled it carefully and gave it to me. So cute. I insisted to share it with him. He agreed happily. While we were eating the apple, several Japanese girl students walked by. Vinegar said he knew one of the girls and began yelling her name. A girl turned to look at him but did not reply. He kept yelling till the girl said in Chinese, "shenjingbing" which means "you are a freak". He was so taken aback with such a response while I was laughing. He was so funny. I like him.

How is Lin? I've planned every detail of seeing him. How I shall run into his open arms and let him squeeze me to death. However, he seldom calls me. Harvey worries me about Lin. He thinks I am too na?ve. Lin is a big cheater. Well, why does he cheat me? I don't think so. No, Lin can never be a cheater. He is kind and lovely.

December 18

Lin came to Zhengzhou yesterday. He was in trouble. He smoked one cigarette after another and asked me whether I would miss him if he disappeared for a long time. I said yes. He looked so helpless and vulnerable last night when I was sitting on his lap in the hotel. I did not ask him what was going on. I did not want to see a general coming from the front humiliated. He was my prince and shall always be. I was so sure that he could do everything successfully. He did not tell me either. He coaxed me to sleep but kept on smoking himself. How could I fall asleep when Lin was suffering something that I cannot share? I lay quietly, gazing at his gloomy face and worried eyes. God, please help Lin! I will be a good girl and obedient lamb. Please take care of Lin for me! What did he mean by disappearing for a long time? Was this the end of our story? See, how cruel life could be!

December 20

I miss you! I miss you!

When I miss you tears would flow.

How I regret not holding your hands and lean on your shoulder for a tiny minute! You always came in the dark and made your fervent love to me. How I regret not slowing you down and holding your hand for a moment! I stopped thinking once your laughing eyes flashed at me. I am so lonely now.

January 10, 2000

It is snowing! The first snow in the year 2000! How exciting! We run out of the classroom and shout happily. Lin, where are you? You love the winter the most. How I want to share this moment with you? Where are you, my heart? Have you forgotten me?

Again, it is Harvey who comes to share my wonder at the first snow. He is a faithful friend. We stand by the bank, watching the pure creatures cover everything with a gentle veil. So quiet. So sweet. Harvey is happy. He holds my cold hands and warms them with his tender lips.

January 11

How excited was I when I received Lin's phone call after I came back to the dorm last night! He was in Xinjiang province. He was sent to the farthest place in China by the reformed company. He was in exile. I told him it was snowing in Zhengzhou and I missed him very much. He said he missed me too and would try to come to Zhengzhou again if possible. My dear prince was in exile! What had he done wrong? He said I was too simple to understand. What I need to do was to study hard and keep in good health.

January 18

Lin had been in Zhengzhou for two days but couldn't spare some time for me. I had waited for his call in the dorm while all the other students were preparing for the exams. Lin was too busy to see me. I went to bed disappointed last night. Pretty soon my roommates began to snort while I lay totally awake, hoping Lin would call me. One channel after another on the radio said good night but Lin did not call. I turned off the radio sadly. Suddenly the phone rang. I rushed to it. It was Lin. He apologized and begged. It was already 12 o'clock. The gate of the building was locked. But I would lie, I would jump, I would do anything to be with Lin. I put on a scarf and ran downstairs. I woke up the gatekeeper and bribed her to open the gate. It was chilly out in the street. His hotel was not far. I decided to walk. While I was walking I remembered that today was Harvey's birthday. I called him and wished him a happy birthday before hand. I walked in the quiet night, so alone. It was snowing. I was walking alone on a snowing night toward my angel. Lin was waiting for me at the lobby. He carried me upstairs and looked at me carefully in his room. My face was red from walking in the fresh air. He kissed it and said I was pretty. I looked at his princely face, his laughing eyes and his thick brows. Thank God, I saw him again. I was too happy to smile. I wept. He kissed my tears tenderly and whispered lots of apologies. The more he said the more I cried. I felt so sorry for us. I cried for my love, my youth and my dear Lin. I felt in my bones that this was going to be the last time for us to be together. How short can beauty last! How deep can a love cut into a human heart! We made love in tears, a slow but lasting love. It was still snowing this morning. He walked me to school. He embraced me once more and walked away. Seven months ago we met on this day and now we had to part. (If I knew I would never be able to hug him again in my life I would rather die in his arm on that snowing morning.)

Chapter Ten

Country Romance

January 27

Another day has passed since I came home for the winter vacation. My village was still backward and dirty. But there was a flame burning in my heart, encouraging me to look forward to the future and look out to the world outside of the poor countryside. Every morning roosters will crow me up to read aloud in the chilly air. I am yearning for a much better and meaningful life. I am willing to strive hard for it.

All my friends, good luck to you.

January 31

I spent the whole day with my second sister yesterday. I began to know her as a married woman after our night talk. She complained about being neglected by her stupid husband who only came home once a month. I met my eldest sister on the street. She was preparing goods for the Spring Festival. She was still so good and poor. I searched my pocket but found nothing to give to my little nephew who was skinny with malnutrition. How I wish all my folks can live a comfortable life! And Lin, how are you now? I can't forget the hard pads in your shoes. They were too small for your big feet. How can you walk in the coldest province of China with those hard pads?

My right foot was frozen under the old quilts. I am sorry for it.

I must do something for my families. I love them so. God father, please bless those who care me. Please look after Lin for me, thanks.

February 1

Another slow and busy day is ending. I am again in bed recording the passing day. I am dying for school life though I love the two little babies. My brother has moved back home with his enlarged family one month ago. They are proud of the newly-born baby boy. I love this tiny soft thing though he has wetted my pants several times. The tiny boy's little sister is a smart and piteous thing. She has just learned to walk. She has to look after herself since her parents and grandparents give all their attention to the male heir. Poor thing, she has to get up as early as my father so that she can drink some milk from his bowl. Her little hands are frozen and are tied up with some cotton. She is always crying which breaks my heart. What can I do for you, little girl? I am her only protector at home but I am too indulged in my love and dream to be a qualified aunt.

February 2

Only when I called and heard your voice did I know how much I miss you. Do you miss me? I am not confident about that. But thank you for being kind in the phone. Lin, keep well in the cold weather.

I happened to see the cards Ben wrote to me on my last birthday. He called me his dearest friend. Thank you, Ben. I sincerely wish you a happy new year and a bright future.

Harvey, what are you doing? I've treated you so unfairly since I met Lin on 18th June, 1999. Do you know how sorry I am for us? You are so good-natured and kind to me, yet I was silly to cry for another man. I think I know you so well that I make fun of you sometimes. Yes, you are too young to let me be proud of your achievement. Harvey, no matter what happens, you are the last one I want to hurt. You are just too dear in my heart. I take your love for me as granted. Only when I saw you sitting with another girl did I realized how I had deprived your right to be a man. Harvey, I am your queen but you are not to be a king. That's the problem with us. I need changes, dreams and a better life but you are so content with the reality. You are too slow for me. I sincerely wish you could grow up in the New Year and give me a pleasant surprise by being a real man.

Lin, compared with Harvey, I know so little about you. I intended to bring you down to earth instead of worshipping you in a dream. I am not sure what it is that stopped me asking you about something I really want to know. Maybe I am afraid of finding you a man as common as everyone else. Then I will be aimless. I will have nothing to fight for. You are my sun. I can't afford to lose your light. You've told me again and again that you love me but I am just not confident about that. You are a mystery that I can't afford to discover. I sincerely hope you can take me seriously though your eyes are always laughing mischievously. Wish you great success with in your sales work in the New Year!

God, my dear Father, I always believe that you are leading me to live this life. Thank you for giving me so many opportunities to enjoy myself. Thank you for giving me so many friends to accompany me on this one-way journey. The Chinese New Year is coming. I sincerely wish you a happy new year.

Chinese New Year

It's about six thirty. Fireworks are cracking near and far, loud and low, quick and slow. The tiny baby boy is crying. My little niece is knocking at my door. She is coming to show off her new clothes. A cannon blows up in the fresh morning air "Dong---ka—!"It is believed that the loudest sound would bring good luck to the owner. My parents used to dry the fireworks under the bed sheet on the clay bed. Now the manufactures have improved their workmanship so that the fireworks are dry and strong. "Dong---ka----!" the whole village, and the whole country is blessed by the thundering sound of fireworks and canons. O, my poor countrymen, my dear villagers, they have so many good wishes for the new year no matter how hard the reality is. May God bless us.

If I am an overseas Chinese many years later, it must be

splendid to watch my motherland from afar on New Year's morning when smoke hovers above this gentle land.

Father came to give me 50 Yuan as the "press age money". I am 22 years old. Father was so proud of me and proud of himself for bring up such a daughter by selling bean curd. I thanked him and would be so happy to give him a hug if I were a westerner. No, I am a Chinese, so I pretend to refuse several times before I put it in my pocket.

The tiny baby is crying again. Maybe he is too eager to express himself. Happy all my countrymen! Happy my dear China!

It's a fine day. The sky is so blue and quiet that I want to melt into this vast sea. There are light clouds kissing the pure sea gently. It is also a slow day. My dear playmates are adults now. Qin is married and Ping is engaged. I am left alone to drink wine with my aging parents. Mother is great. She tries to cheer me up and spread a table of dishes for lunch. My sisters have long been married into other families. My brother prefers to stay with his wife in another room. I am the only child they have now. Father would talk to me in a childish way sometimes, forgetting I am 22 years old. I want to go nowhere but mother's warm bed after lunch. I sit there reading in the sun which is shining on the new wall papers and new quilts through glass window pane. I feel a little lonely and sad. What is Lin doing? Is he giving New Year's greeting by kneeling in front of ancestor tablets? I can't help smiling at such a picture—my handsome prince kneeling down, touching the ground with his head, and standing up with hands over his head. No man can escape this ritual in the countryside. Though brother complained about his sore knees last year, he still went out to "kowtow" early in the morning. The Spring Festival wouldn't be so solemn and interesting without this ritual. Some drying bloodstreams identify with the main currents this morning and then flow to the ancient sea joyfully. Many conflicts and quarrels would be pardoned when men recognize their ancestors in this thousand -year- old way.

January 2(Lunar calendar)

It is a busy day. Many relatives come to give New Year's greetings. They come with bags of special food (mainly steamed bread and fried noodles), have one meal with us, chat with my parents and then leave for another family. I can't help thinking what Lin would do if we get married one day. O, it is so far away. I shouldn't think of it now. God, please remind Lin of me. Thanks.

My niece Apricot is interrupting me with absurd questions. I have to stop now. Bye, all those who love me.

January 3

I am touched to tears again and again when I reread the old letters my friends wrote to me years ago. Rong called me her "dear friend" which was not usual in rural China. I was so important to her in those years. How foolish was I to neglect her naive but pure feelings! Maybe this is just a way of life. We pass by carelessly without reading each other's heart and try to love our friends in our selfish way. Thank you, Rong.

Then came Qin's neat writings to wish "happy the new years!" to me in primary school when I was 11years old. My best playmate is a mother now. I didn't know why I wanted to cry when I sat with her yesterday afternoon. Her baby was crying. She tried to calm him down and thrust her nipple into his searching little mouth. "She is a woman now" I thought to myself and wept inside.

I have kept these letters for years. Worms have woven nests on some yellow pages which hold so much love and friendship.

The world is changing, so am I. It's good to look back sometimes to find how true I have loved and how hard a road I have walked. Clinton wrote so many letters to encourage me in high school but he is not my flag any more. He is not the one I can look up to, but I sincerely thank him for everything he did to urge me forward years ago.

I drink a lot of wine these days not out of happiness but out of unbearable sadness. I am on the edge of destroying something. I want to forget all the unhappy past. I want to be drunk so that nothing matters to me anymore.

My brother is also drinking a lot these days. He is under so much pressure. Three children open their mouths to him for food. He is growing gloomy and weak, my dear brother. He gets himself drunk and sobs in his room. God, I kiss your gentle hands and beg you to take care of my brother.

I must check my feelings for Lin. I am waking up from the long dream that I've been making since I saw the first white pear flower in my wonderland. I've done lots of foolish things. Now

I need the assurance of love and a home. Most of my girlfriends have found their nests, be it rich or poor. And Patricia alone is still reaching her arms out for a splendid dream. Will someone give me a little love? Will someone draw me a blueprint? Will someone lend me a shoulder when I am tired? Will someone do all these?

February8 (Solar calendar)

I am eager to go back to school. I am tired of this slow and lazy life at home. I don't need to do anything and so I achieve nothing. No, this is not the right life I want. I am eager to take risks and to succeed. No one cares about what I am thinking. Only Qin said I was mature now but she was too occupied with her crying baby to listen to stories. I'm so lonely and tired. Then I think of Vinegar—the funny boy I met at the library. He said once that he decided to cultivate me into his wife. A wife? Vinegar's wife? Ha-ha-ha I laughed while he boasted about buying me a mink coat and high-heeled boots. He said I shouldn't do any part-time job this year. I must concentrate on the postgraduate exams. But how can I stop working when the load on my shoulder is getting heavier and heavier? I'm not a child anymore. I need to work to study and study well. I must succeed.

I can't marry Harvey. That's for sure. I must let him know this without hurting him too much. Lin is like a moon to me, something I can appreciate but can't get.

Father came in to give some delicacies to his little daughter. He was so ready to please me and was most happy when I played my role as his little girl by kicking shuttlecocks or skipping a rope or doing upside down against the wall. They stake such a great expectation on me. I've worked hard but sometimes I can't help enjoying myself with romantic imaginations. I've been crazy for one boy after another. I am desperate to look for a person who can be my beacon light. Lin is such a man but I am not confident about his love. He seldom talks about future with me. Maybe I've chosen the wrong person. No, I can't be wrong. I can't afford to be wrong now. Harvey can't understand this. That's why I don't want to waste time persuading him to give me up. He's still a child. Even if Lin doesn't love me he can still be a light to encourage me.

My niece Apricot came to let me forgive her. I had long forgotten why I was angry at her. I pardoned this cute little thing at once. Nothing can't be forgiven.

February 9

I called Lin this evening. He sounded very unhappy. I finished the call quickly though it meant so much to me. He was having dinner at home. He was unhappy and was drinking. I felt so weak and hurt after the call. I walked on the empty street, not hearing what Apricot was telling me. The moon was so quiet and remote. Was Lin sharing the same moon with me? Why couldn't he feel my pain? Apricot asked me what the matter was. Why was I so silent after the call? I told her my heart ached. Yes, my heart, it was beating so reluctantly as if there was no hope, no future, and no aim for me to strive for any more. This photo doesn't have any meaning any more if Lin cares for me so little. I asked Apricot for a match and decided to burn it. Alas, look at those shining eyes, how can I bear not be able to see them again! No one can tell me how I can feel better or at least not so lonely and depressed. My niece agreed to burn it. I asked her why. She said because Lin was not friendly to you. I asked her why he was not friendly to me. She said because Lin did not like you. I was startled at her simple truth but still tried to win her over. I said maybe he was just unhappy when I called. So he was not in the mood to talk. Then shall I forgive him? Yes, she said, you should forgive him. I asked why. She said because you liked him. Gosh, how can she know anything about like or not. I asked her again why. She frowned and said firmly, "because you like him but he doesn't like you". O, what a child! What a strange logic but maybe she is right. I was so discouraged by Apricot's philosophy that I had to drink wine to forget the pain. "Hold fast to the dream" these words jumped into my mind when I asked myself what I should do if Lin turned out to be a married man with a daughter. God, dear father, shall I give up? Or should I hold fast to this dream? Maybe time is the best judge. One thing for sure is that I can't desert Lin when he is in trouble now. God, please bless Lin. I hope it is not me who brings him bad luck.

Maybe he is a real man who makes me grow up by leaving me to face the harsh realities alone. Before I am sure what's in his mind I still choose to believe his love. So dear Lord, please help Lin to overcome his failure in his business so that he will have time and mood to think of me. Good night, Lin. If you see me in your dream please be kind to me for I have forgiven your coldness on the phone.

God bless all those who deserve it.

February 10

It's really a busy day. Several "distinguished" relatives came to see their uncle and niece who was a college student now. My father was so excited about the coming of the big potatoes as if the king had come to see his poor slaves. But where were these rich people when father had to beg house after house for my tuition? I received their sudden attention paid to me coldly. They wouldn't have come to see their poor bean-curd-maker uncle if he did not happen to have a daughter who was smart enough to be the first one in town to go to college. Father and I have made a right investment. It's a long-term investment. Only patient and formidable people can make a profit from it. That is my education. I must work hard and climb higher and higher on the social ladder.

My eldest sister came especially to see me. She dreamt that I went to see her but couldn't find her house after about 4 year's absence. So she got up early and came to invite me to her house. My dear sister had prepared my favorite food. Her son Lele ran all the way to make sure that I hadn't gone back to school.

I went to the wild field with Lele and Apricot. I allowed them to climb trees, to roll in the soft dirt and to make stories with their marvelous imaginations. I was surprised to find the date valley where Qin, Ping and I spent our childhood was replaced by an express highway. Things are changing so quickly. I lingered in the field till darkness, trying to remember every detail of this childhood Eden. Ai, no more, within a blink of eyes, innocent years are gone!

February 11

I felt good after the long nap and the romance with Lin flashed in my mind. He stood at the north gate, waiting for a girl in a long skirt and with a book in her left hand. That was our sign. I came downstairs wondering who was the man that called this noon to sing me that silly song *My heart is too soft*. He did not tell me who he was or how he got my number. Instead he asked to see me at 3 p.m. I went to the north gate and looked around but did not see anyone in blue jeans. Who else would sing that kind of silly song except a stupid boy in jeans? I thought to myself. Well, there was only one man in the hot sun. He was too handsome and too manly to be "that boy". O my God, he was walking to me. I tried to look indifferent while he was sweeping me with those laughing eyes. It was Lin. He came from Heaven on that Double Fifth's Day when people were paying their tribute to the dead. He stole my heart and ran away. But I am in a good mood now. I prefer to see the unearthly beauty in our romance. There is something mysterious about it. I am hooked. No matter what happened or will happen I thank God for this divine accident.

The village is quiet again under the black veil of evening.

Good night, all my friends.

February 12

I went to see my eldest sister today. They are living in that decaying house. The only new thing in her simple room is the scarf I bought her last year. She kept it in a case and wore it only on real big occasions. My nephew Lele was having a hard time at school. He ran away from school several times and couldn't catch up with other students. I believe it has something to do with the teaching method in the countryside. Students are not encouraged or cared for. They were like weeds, left alone in the rain to die or to live. What can I do to help them? My sister's little daughter Swallow liked me instantly. She followed me everywhere and cried piteously when I had to leave. O, my poor children, how skinny you are! It's a sin for me to indulge in my love story when my folks are striving to keep alive.

February 14

Only when I wrote the date down did I realize it was Valentine's Day. How are you, all the boys who have ever loved me? And how are you the one I love?

I slept for three hours in the afternoon and woke up to find a dark world. I was in a good mood and went up to the roof with my little niece. There, in the open air I sang and danced. I belonged to the mysterious night and delicate nature this evening. I had no love nor hate for humans on the lover's day. I was strangely calm and peaceful.

What is love? It's the eternity of life. Our forefathers believed that by bonding two persons together with law they could produce and preserve love. Thus comes marriage which shows to the world that they belong to each other and they have come down to everyday life from imagination. Sometimes even the greatest love may die when life becomes too true. Yet love surely does not grow in the darkness. It must breathe under the sunshine to enjoy the delicious details of human society and the wonders of nature.

There is an idiom in Chinese called "Ye Gong Hao Long". "Ye" is the surname of a man; "Gong" means sir; "hao" means like; "Long" is a dragon which is a powerful animal in Chinese culture. A certain Mr. Ye boasts that he loves dragon more than any other things in the world. He draws it every day and engraves it on the columns that support his house. The dragon in the heaven is so pleased and touched on hearing this man's fervent love and decides to pay Mr. Ye a visit. He twists and flies and swims in the sky, heading for Mr. Ye's house. When this dragon fan looks up at this marvelous animal, he is so frightened that he tries to hide himself. The dragon is so excited about his fan that he follows Mr. Ye and tries to touch the frightened fan with his long mouth. Mr. Ye falls on the ground, dead. Some people make up their minds to pursue pure love, but when it leads to marriage they turn and try to escape. Why is marriage so terrible? Maybe it is really not the right way to test love. Maybe the lovers themselves do not take care to lubricate their beliefs when frictions of everyday life hurt each other.

February 14th is the day for those who are still "talking about" love to put their two hearts together and check whether the hearts can beat as one. It is a day for them to "think about" sacrificing something for love.

Thank God for reminding me of this important and special

day. Please pour good luck to the friends who love me kindly and to the one I've chosen to follow. Thank you, dear Father; you must be watching me somewhere in this vast universe for my tears are stinging my nose for your selflessness.

Lin, keep well. No matter what happens I pray the best for you. Sleep, my dear. Be kind to me in your dream and love me in your heart.

February 17

It's ten past three in the early morning. The day has finally come. My neighbor boiled ten eggs for me to take on the journey. I am blessed. I do hope that I can repay my dear villagers one day.

Loud noise comes from distant trucks. They are building the express highway which runs through my happy valley. Several hours later I will leave the wildness of countryside for a busy and crowded city. How are Patrick and Amy now? They are the first westerners many Chinese students have ever seen and also the first challengers to our oriental mind. They encourage us to be creative, honest and brave. The very word of "creativity" is dynamic enough to inspire our sleeping senses. May God bless them!

Be it happy or miserable, sweet or bitter, good or bad, what's past has passed; be it glorious or disappointing, promising or depressing; great or small, what's going to happen has not taken place. So treasure what we have now no matter it's time or achievement or love.

Chapter Eleven

Struggle for Air

February20

The beginning of this semester is unexpectedly sad. The results of last exam were so bad that I almost lost confidence in myself. What is my future? Which school shall I select to do my master's degree? Or which major? Ai, won't somebody come to draw me a clear blueprint?

Maybe I should stop keeping a diary. Every day is like dancing on the sharp edge of a dagger. I must smother the fervent and insane fire burning for Lin. I need to stop thinking.

April 22

I lost him at last. I called him again and again till a stranger answered Lin's number. He said he knew nothing about Lin. If I call this number again, he will cut my throat. What's wrong? I got frantic. Has Lin been cheating me all the time? Have I really met a man named Lin or was it a fancy on that Ghost's Day? O my dear God, what is it that you are trying to show me? Is it love or infatuation or an empty dream? Who am I? Am I a real person? I'm so confused now. I took out Lin's only photo and tore it into pieces. Gone, those killing eyes!

May 4

So much has changed. I've picked up some virtues as well as vices during the long run. I've spent much time with myself since that fatal blow from Lin's mobile. The black clouds have passed in my college life. What romance! What devotion! I have to grow up after so much rain to reach out for sunshine. Lin is a thunder to my sprouting trust in love. He has given me unprecedented beauty and torture. I've searched all the books I have and all the knowledge I have accumulated to look for a sound explanation for his sudden disappear. Why must I lose him? Why isn't he brave enough to tell me face to face? I've searched my heart for an answer. Have all those long letters from me hurt him? How? I avoided using any harsh words in the letter. Maybe my love is too strong for him. He knows himself as a common man while I insist that he should be my perfect angel. I've frightened him away with too many splendid dreams. Maybe he thinks I am a lunatic who loves talking in the moon light. It's painful to realize that he doesn't need me anymore. But what is even worse is to find that I've given in so much to a "fairy tale" and only to find that we are hiding something from each other.

I was so pious and vulnerable to my loving angel that I've lived a strange life. I've changed so much and there is no possibility to erase all the tears, fears and doubts to go back to my innocent years. Something is lost but I can't make it up. I must be a complete person again. I mustn't be afraid of this world.

May 20

Lin has left only a name in my memory now. His picture has become a blur. I've busied myself with my English study so that I won't be able to review the painful past. If there are some cheaters around us or even playing important roles in our life, we can do nothing about it. Girls are living in a dream where feelings are pure, hearts are kind and intentions are noble.

Father called me this noon to tell me that they had received my letter. He reminded me again that I had my root in the wildness where no one would reject me or cheat me.

Lin, it is getting harder and harder for me to form a picture of you in my mind. Where are you now? Do you still remember me? Are you true to me? Something has happened to you and has changed you. I wish you were as strong and promising as ever.

May 22

I had my pictures taken in a Photoshop last week. I was so surprised to look at a different girl in the pictures when I went to fetch them today. I was made up with lipstick, false eyelashes and whitening powder. I wore three gowns: a white one, a green one and a red one. I looked sideways, bent down, spread the long tails of the gown and smiled. O, I can be so pretty, so charming and so feminine! I ran into the dorm and shouted till all my sleeping roommates rolled up to appreciate a BEAUTIFUL Patricia.

May 26

It began to rain after supper. The sky is grey and high. I like this kind of mood, vast and remote.

I am considering making a special gift to Amy, Patrick and Alta. They are leaving China this summer vacation. I want to thank them for the years they have shared with me. They appeared in the most precious and innocent period of my life. Their kindness and good manners leave a deep impression on my mind. I hope to do a good job in the final exam to repay their hard work.

I wonder what Lin is doing now. Maybe he will call me when he feels confident and proud again. Maybe he will never call. It makes no difference to me. I only hope that sometimes a gentle chord in his heart may be struck to remind the affection we ever had for each other and how precious it once was.

June 4

I dreamt of a tree with big flowers among its green leaves. The flowers were blue, white and pink. Branches were sweeping the slope under the heaviness of huge flowers. I was coming down the hill and was so happy to see the unearthly flowers. I sang at the top of my voice and knelt down to touch the inviting petals. I was a lamb, wandering in the beautiful Eden, carefree and happy. I woke up with a chirping bird in my memory. I took my bag and went to the library. I walked across the grassland, the rose garden and the golden river, calm and happy. Those beautiful episodes of dreams flashed in my mind: sunshine, flowers, temples, mountains, grass and muddy slope. How my heart longs for a life with natural beauty and carefree love!

June 8

There is something in me that urges me to express myself in words though the low mark in the written exam has discouraged me greatly. I just have to write. I know myself by writing and I write more smoothly when love and nature master my wild imagination. I've tried to read the text books and write dry reports but, O, I can't force myself. Patricia is as stubborn as a mule though she was born in the horse year. I spent the whole week on the fifth floor of the library, reading about the great cities of the world such as Rome, London, Moscow, Paris etc. Every city has a long history and every history is a peculiar culture. I read and thought and imagined till my heart was taken away by the fabulous pictures and mysterious destinies of these cities.

Chapter Twelve

Who is the Queen?

July 5

Summer vacation starts. I am home now, wondering how to study efficiently with little children running about and screaming. The poor, dirty and lazy countryside life made me want to escape as soon as I dragged my trunk out of the bus. But this is my home. I have to put up with it and concentrate on my study. Two months are long enough to make a great change.

July 7

I am listening to VOA now which is the only link I have to the outside world. I have taken home the English versions of the four classic Chinese novels---*Scholars, A Dream in the Red Mansions, Monkey King* and *All men are Brother*---sand Emerson's essays. I am eager to become fat at one bite.

I think of Harvey tonight. He has been very patient and kind to me. He took me out for a walk and bought me little gifts when I was so hurt by Lin's sudden disappear. He never complained when

I let my steam off on him. I cursed him, pinched him, insulted him but he always came to see me during weekends. Sometimes I let him hold my hands; sometimes I walked meters away from him; sometimes I cried in his arms and sometimes I hated him for being kind to me. My roommates said I was a silly girl, throwing away a pure jade but crying for a broken bubble. They pitied Harvey and urged me to date him again. Harvey, Harvey, I am so sorry. I know I am wrong, I am selfish, I am mean, but, why aren't you Lin?

July 18

A cousin of mine came to see me this evening. We had a long talk. The world was quite a different one in his eyes. After watching my photos he said I was too defenseless and naive. He warned me that to survive in this fierce world I had to be stone-hearted and shrewd.

Well, maybe he is right. He has experienced a lot since he ran away from school at 13. He is like a poor dandy who is abandoned by his girls when his pocket is empty. He has a strange way to make money. Sometimes he seems rich and confident on his shining motorbike. Sometimes he is as depressed as a beggar. His parents have given him up. He seldom goes home even on the Spring Festival which breaks my uncle's heart. He only goes home twice a year to see my grandparents. He would buy my grandma soft and sour delicacies and my grandpa spicy food. His love for the elderly people is such a contrast to his cynical philosophy that he becomes a riddle. My parents always say this dandy is doomed to end up in jail. He is so brave, free and lonely. My dandy cousin looked at my pictures and said I was still such a little girl at 22. He said the stupid blood of this family had passed on to me. If I want to succeed, I must rebel against something inside me--- cowardice, honesty and stupidity. My father was so alarmed at his mad talk that he did not invite my dandy cousin to stay for the night. He jumped on his motor and disappeared into the darkness.

July 19

I feel dizzy the whole day. Every time I stand up, darkness covers my eyes. My health is decaying. I will buy some vitamins tomorrow.

I am so weak now, sick, lost and sad. I need to be alive and active to prevent my heart from breaking down. I've been reading Japanese these days. How can I study the language well when I am so sick of its beastly people? Every time I open the book I will think of the Nanjing massacre and the bloody documentaries I saw in school. Why did they invade my country and kill my people? What were they? Humans or beasts? But I have to study Japanese if I want to do postgraduate work. It's a shame.

July 27

I went to see a doctor. She tested my blood and said the pressure was too low. No wonder I feel weak and dizzy these days. I am neglected at home. No one cooks. I go hungry. The thousand-year-old battle between mother-in-law and daughter-in-law renewed at once when my brother's family came back from hiding in the fields. Mother refuses to cook because she is "elderly", the respected and the queen of the house. My sister-in-law doesn't cook either for she is NOT hungry until my brother comes home from the gold mountain once a month! I am too obsessed with books and too angry to cook. So I go hungry at my own home. Well, maybe it is not my home any more, especially after quarrelling with the queen of the house.

I bought some medicine and found it was made in Jilin where Mr. Turning was born. Mr. Turning? I laughed to myself. What a dream with this man! Damn you! And damn Lin too! No one cared about me when I was so down and down. They fooled me and left. I was too naive and silly to meet their desire. I beautified them in my heart only to help them fool myself. I will make my fortune and beat them sooner or later. I am old enough to face the reality and take good care of myself. I must make some headway in my study. I must beat all those who fool me and discourage me. Even God is so naughty and bad. I curse you my God. I entrust myself to you and you only play with me. My life can't hold so much despised tears. I am wearing out. I need to rebel. Enough is enough! Enough is the bitter, humble, silent and lonely self-torture! I need to taste a little bit of sweetness from life.

August 5

I came to stay with my second sister a week ago. She was angry to find me hungry and depressed at home and asked me to stay with her. She is busy running a department store of her husband's family but always walks home at noon to bring me some delicious food such as beef or noodle or chicken. I get up early to run in the wide national street near her house. I'm getting fit now. Thank you, dear sister. My brother came to see me once. He is getting thinner and thinner without regular meals in the gold mountain. I am so worried about him. Time has changed us. The sisters and brother are not fighting children any more. They have their commitment to their own small families yet I am still alone to pursue an invisible future.

August 10

Lin is an integral part of my planned future. Whenever I meet some words I like I will think whether it sounds beautiful with a surname Lin. When I read " 青梅 " this afternoon in the Japanese text book my heart throbbed. " 青梅 " means green plum in English. It would surely be a wonderful name for my daughter. Lin Qingmei---a small wood of green plum trees. Good! How I want a gentle, delicate and sweet daughter with Lin's long eyelashes and my soft hair!

August 11

I've been in town only for two weeks but I long for the countryside. I miss my little nieces and tiny nephew at home. Only now do I feel how attached I've become to my sister's house. She just made a new screen for the door to my room. It is in the shape of butterflies which are made of used bags of instant noodle. My dear sister does not know how to express her love for me. We are not westerners who can hug and kiss. What a shame! Even I can't say thank you to her. It would be most odd to say thank you to family members. She put it on in the morning and I declared that I wanted to go home tomorrow. How cruel am I! I've stayed 12 days here but it is as if I just came down from my brother's motorbike with my school bag. My sister received me happily and cleaned a room for me. Now the house begins to look alive but I have to leave. It looks funny but I really can't hold back my tears. It is the first time I have shared so many days with my sister since she got married five years ago. The first is also the last intimate contact for I am not going to come back. I will miss my little room. And the new butterfly curtain will always be in my memory to remind me how much my sister loves me.

August 12

I am back home now. There is still half a month before I go back to school. I'm restless now. It's so easy for me to get tired of a place except my school. Time is really a pill, a pain-killer pill. With time going by we have to realize that there are things that we just can't get and have to forget and make peace with the world.

August 16

Evening comes. I went upstairs to walk on the roof. I felt so uncertain about my future. I want to draw the bamboo strips in a temple to have my fortune told. I do hope Lin can suddenly appear again in the new semester.

Why do I lose interest in study? Because I lose interest in the present life and a new life is too far away. I'm suffering from chronicle depressions. I've turned from an optimistic girl to a pessimistic woman ever since Lin's sudden failure. I need to recover from this nightmare gradually. I begin to doubt whether he really read the long letters written from my heart and posted with borrowed money. I have to record the beautiful past again and again to liberate myself from the sour present. I've forgotten how to laugh from the bottom of my heart since that snowing morning when Lin hugged me the last time.

August 18

Suddenly I realize that what I should value the most in a person is his attitude towards life and personality. Lin is surely an excellent man who is striving forward. Harvey is gentle and promising. I should be proud of knowing such persons and having their care. God is love, unconditional and unreasonable.

August 19

I spent the late afternoon on the roof. I thought a lot while listening to the murmur of nodding trees and summer bugs. I love this world. I have read some books and have had some general impression about some countries------the US, childish and lovable; the UK, cold and noble; China, loving and heavy; Russia, hard-working; Japan, determined and extreme; Greek and Italy, sacred and romantic; Ireland, rash and passionate; Australia, tall and raw; Africa, strong, black and happy. I find that every nation is an ideal as well as a reality. If I fail the postgraduate exam to the Foreign Affairs College, I will surely succeed in the next exam aiming at British culture in Shanghai International Studies University.

Little Apricot is like my tail. She follows me everywhere even to the toilet. If only every parent can treat children like a real human being instead of shouting at them for some strange excuses that children can never understand! Children are as fresh and vulnerable as flowers.

August 20

Autumn has come. It's still dark outside at 6 am. I lie in bed thinking of that strange dream. I dreamed of huge blocks of cloud. This time they did not look like flowers but turtles and tanks. They were cold and solemn. When I was sitting on a short wall worshipping the powerful clouds, the boy I loved secretly in high school came on a bike. He saluted me and said, "Comrade Liu, would you please show me the way to the heaven?"I murmured something while he lowered his head and kissed my lips. My heart was filled with joy. I wanted to say "thank you" but he was gone. Isn't it a strange dream? Then I think of all my boys who I have loved. The first boy who strikes my heart is my little prince. We used to live in the same lane. He is only one month older than me. It is said that my sister once bit his mother for taking her little sister away. My sister mistook him for me because we were very alike. I began to think of him a lot when we went to primary school. I liked him the most when he scratched his big head stupidly but could not answer the teachers' questions. I would peep over the short wall when he was whipped by his father and hid myself quickly when he looked in my direction. It seemed as if we could sense each other's existence though he only touched me once. That was in grade two. I walked up to him shamelessly and he touched my big round face when the whole class was throwing paper planes and shouting merrily. I liked him so much that I would encourage myself in the darkness by chanting his name. "My prince! My prince! My prince! "I chanted while running to fasten the gate and ran back to my room again. Though we looked alike, he was not as half smart as me. I went on to a key middle school while he quitted after graduation. We were 13 when his house moved to the other end of the village and I went to town for middle school. He would come to give New Year's greeting every year and take the chance to see me. I would look into those familiar eyes but could not find the assurance I need. We are walking on two different roads and the distance between us is getting wider and wider. I am moving further away from the village while he is still toiling and hewing on this poor land. Bye-bye my dear little prince! We can't have each other though we were born so close together. Then I met a boy names Long in middle school. He used to wear a set of green uniform and scarlet shirt. He would stand by the window and stare at my seat while I was too terrified to breathe. I buried my head deep in the books till the bell rang and he went into his classroom. One winter morning I was running upstairs to the classroom while he appeared. I stopped abruptly and walked slowly by so that I looked more lady-like. He roared. When I was drawing pictures in my first diary, my desk mate told me someone was waiting for me on the first floor. I wiped my running nose and went down to see who it was. It was Long's boy friend. I ran back to the dorm before he could speak to me. Silly girl, what were you afraid of? Why did you avoid talking to the boy you like? Because teachers said only bad girls "talk about love" in middle school. Oh, what a shame! We did not exchange a single word though I had seen him so many times in my dream. Then we graduated. I furthered my study in the key senior middle school in a city while he became a miner in the gold mountain in the little town. Thus ended my second romantic story. I went to the No.1 senior middle school when I was 15 years old and fell in love at first sight with the boy named Jin. He was the student speaker when we were having the welcoming meeting in the hall. He tossed his fluffy hair, waved his strong arms and spoke every word as clearly as gospel. My heart tinged and I knew it was shot by Cupid's arrow. He looked strangely beautiful in the morning sun under the red national flag. I missed him every day during the three years at school. His name was a special dish for the girls when we had our meals in the dingy dorm. I never talked about him openly. He was too sacred to share with others. We were divided into the same class in grade two when all the students had to choose between arts and science. He was the monitor of the arts' class and I was the one who always got the best score in English exams. I cherished his name in my dreams though I never had the courage to talk to him. I wandered on the playground and sang sad love songs till my friends gave me a nickname "romantic fairy". Being an ordinary-looking girl I didn't expect much from him, a stolen glance or two were enough for me. But one night when I looked up from my homework to steal a glance at my white prince, a pair of scorching eyes met mine. He was resting his head on crossed arms and looking affectionately at me. My face turned red and my heart stopped beating. I bit my thumb not knowing what to do next. He cleared his throat and began to sing: my love is known to her, my love is naked to her……O, that moment should be frozen so that I could take it wherever I go. But again I was a coward. I did not meet his searching eyes after that most beautiful night. I couldn't afford to love him openly. I was too poor, too humble and too timid. I cried a million times when he dared to play with other girls but walked quickly away when he tried to approach me. He was like the sun. I would die in his glory if I was too close to him. So I chose to shy away though I kissed his names in my diaries. Then came the graduation. I went to a college in Zhengzhou while he failed the college entrance exam and started a business in his hometown. My third romantic story ended in the same tragic way. When I met Lin at the north gate of Zhengzhou University I thought he was my cupid in high school and fell in love with him as fervently as I first saw Jin waving his arms in the morning sun. Where is Lin now? My beautiful boys go their own way one by one, leaving me alone to wonder and wander in this mysterious world. I hope God can help me focus my life on one person. I will fulfill all my dreams, new and old, through my love for him.

August 22

Today's my birthday. It's raining heavily now.

Yesterday father bought some beef and eggs for my birthday. I had mentioned that I wanted to have some beef but I couldn't bear the smell when I tried it last night. So I refused to eat any of it. This morning mother fried the eggs for me but again I couldn't bear the smell. I forced in one mouth of the beef again to please my father but vomited. It seemed that I had suddenly lost interest in eating. Father was so enthusiastic about my birthday, but was upset by my cold remark about the food he bought. I am sorry. God, why am I so cold to the ones who care me most? Maybe I am made of grass and flower petals. So I should feed on plants instead of animals.

Darkness is covering the earth now. I feel restless and hostile. Something in me has changed since I knew Lin.

August 23

I went to see my eldest sister with mother. My sister felt so privileged to have us as her guests that she fried some eggplants for us. The condition was getting worse in her family. They had to borrow money to send the two kids to school. But my sister still looked so content and happy. She went to church once a week and found condolence in Jesus. She was raising pigs, chickens and sheep in her small yard. She grew all kinds of crops on their dry land. What else can she do as a traditional Chinese woman farmer? When they still could not make ends meet, they would make peace with fate and stay happy though half hungry. After lunch we went to see an old opera which was played on a simple clay stage built in the field. This was like the one I saw in my grandpa's village--- old people, old play, simple stage and simple happiness. I bought a lucky string with one Yuan and wore it around my neck. I wanted to be blessed by the country god and be connected to the fading past.

August 24

I am upset after a long nap. Life is so undesirable. I have nothing to eat when I am hungry but don't have a good appetite when meals are ready. I want to eat an ice cream but when I see it I feel sick. It seems that I have lost interest in eating but I AM hungry. I am so annoyed at a strange Patricia that tears rush out. Suddenly I decide that I have had enough of home life. Only children are bonding the two families together. The two queens of the old family and my brother's new family are always at silent war. Mother would rather play poker than cook. She doesn't like my sister-in-law "sitting idly and put flowers in her hair". When my sister-in-law really cooks, she doesn't like her dishes which are not spicy or cooked or salty enough. So after a week's trying to please the old queen the new queen declares one day that she is not hungry and wouldn't cook any more. So father, the three kids and I go hungry at our own home and are too guilty to eat when the old queen descends from her throne to cook once a day. I am not interested in cooking and won't waste time eating when exams are drawing near. I feel tired of this kind of life. There is no love that can encourage my family members to think for each other. I think the two families should separate and live their own lives when they don't match. What's the point in living together when we all have to go hungry? For a "united" face before the neighbors? Pooh, face is nothing compared with my health! There is no one who really cares about me. I am old enough to look after myself. What if I am not in the mood to look after myself? Bad luck, I have to be neglected. I feel out of place at home. So I spend most of my time on the roof where I have lonely walks, talk nonsense to myself and fall asleep in the hot sun. One day my friend Qin came to see me. I was so happy at first but annoyed at last. Her baby was crying all the time. She had to shake him and move about all the time. I put the good luck string bought in the village temple around his neck. I should tie some money to the string as customs goes but I was penniless. So I just tied the string around his neck and then saw them off. Now what do I have? I am abandoned by my queens, by my brother, by my two sisters and by my best old friend! I sit on the roof crying. I am as helpless and lonely as a child. No one wants to take me home. Harvey loves me but there is something missing in his love. I have to ask him then he can see what I need. I have to shed tears to let him know that I am not happy. I have to frown hard to show him that I am confused and lost. Is there a person who is myself and my God? Who knows surely what I am crying for and what I am afraid of? Is there really such a person? If there is, I'm ready to entrust my life in his hand and feel so gentle to this world. If there isn't such a person, I will have to live my life violently. Don't let me lead your forward, Harvey. Give me a little surprise by being a man.

God father, am I very bad tonight? What do you intend to let me do by making me so unhappy for such a long time? There is only three days left before I leave this hungry home. God, make me behave like a good child. I'll leave and won't come back till I find my love and my inner peace.

God father, you must be tired since you have looked after such a girl for so long. Please rest. My heart is gentle for you.

August 26

I just came back from the hair-dresser with my sleepy niece. She is sound asleep beside me now. I'm sorry for the trouble I've brought to her. I had my hair curled tonight. Now my hair is soft and shining. I must take care of it with good shampoo.

Mother did not scold me for coming back with stars above my head. She grows tender to me when my days at home are numbered. This afternoon I packed my books and clothes. While looking at the empty room I felt a sudden pain, nameless yet profound.

Thank God for the day. Good night, the loving world.

August 28

It's about 6 a.m. now. The day has finally come for me to go back to school ----a place that holds so many of my expectations. Father borrowed the tuition for me. My brother thrust 100 Yuan in my bag when my sister-in-law was not present. I wanted to refuse but couldn't. My brother would be hurt if I did not accept his token of love. He insisted that he should accompany me to the railway station in town and bought ten big apples for my roommates. My niece Apricot got up early too. She was excited about going back to school just like me. Another Patricia is growing but much happier.

It's five o'clock in the afternoon. I am on the train now. It's raining outside. The raindrops are crawling down the window glass like tears. Why is heaven crying? What is a world waiting for me? I pray for a world where there are no tears, no heartbreaks or self-consciousness which will kill my confidence. I pray that I can see Lin one more time or at least hear his voice. I am calm now since I've learned to accept the reality. Life is not a comedy or tragedy. Life is what we respect it. Now another world is opening its arms to me.

Chapter Thirteen

A Room of One's Own

August 29

I can't believe it. I was one day late for school! I remembered the wrong date. Six and Harvey had already moved all my belongings back from the classroom. The reunion was a happy and peaceful one.

Six bought me a very nice schoolbag as a birthday present. She and Dragon wrote a birthday letter to me. I will read it when I am upset later so that I can feel being loved in this world again. My roommates told me Yangzi came to see me when I was still at home. I wondered what was happening to her now. She is so alone and desperate. I hope our friendship can warm each other when we feel helpless sometimes. I wish there would be a happy marriage waiting for her.

Rui came to see me just now. She bought me a book named *Moment in Peking* by Lin Yutang. I was very shy and touched at the words she wrote on the first page of the book: Tell me what I can do for you. I would do it no matter how far I am from you. I don't know what else I may ask from a friend. The book is very thick. It must be very expensive. Her tuition was totally borrowed from her kind granduncle. Why would she spend so much money on a book? Because she knows I love this book and she loves me. God, I am so grateful to you. At the very beginning of this year I've received so much love. How shall I thank you enough? I am loved and I am able to love. Don't be unhappy anymore.

September 1

I spent a wonderful evening in the library last night. I set my mind free and opened the whole picture of a new life for myself. I will continue to learn Chinese painting if possible; I will study Japanese to such a level that I can read original novels. Then there are political theories that I must memorize for the postgraduate exam. I need to read the thick book at least once. Then there is the detailed study of English every day and the life I need to live happily and fully. I've spent 100 Yuan during these three days. I hope to find a well-paid part-time job soon. I feel like a peaceful angel walking back to the dorm to the slow song melting in the air. God, thank you for the calmness you give me. I am still not on the track to any clear aim but I am seeking. Bless your child, God.

September 2

When I was eating a big watermelon with my roommates, tears stung my nose. Six bought the watermelon for us with the money she earned by collecting empty plastic bottles on the street. Six, a garbage collector? I tried not to link her with such a profession. How could we eat the watermelon since we secretly laughed at her when she put the empty bottles under her bed? She is poor but she is BEAUTIFUL.

Harvey asked me out last night. He was planning to buy me a birthday present though his tuition was all borrowed. People are so kind to me. Thank God, I am so blessed.

September 3

I was reading *Moment in Peking* when it began to rain. If not for my dear book I would rather stay in the rain.

I read a long article about Liao Xiaoyi this morning. She is a philosopher and environmentalist. I think there is something in her that I need to learn. Philosophy is not something cold or useless to the common good. She puts her philosophy into action. She came back to China after studying in the US and has devoted her heart to protect the decaying environment in China. She is a philosopher but not a book worm. She does not sit on the clouds and separates herself from common people. She comes down to take care of the public good. I am so proud of her. I also find that the western style of education liberates not only people's mind but their hands. That is a big difference from the Chinese education. The western people not only talk they DO.

When I was reading in the garden I saw several petals of China roses sliding down to the ground. They were tragic but beautiful.

September 5

An ambulance whistled by in the rain. A chill ran through my mind and body. Is something bad happening to Lin? I still remember that deep fear at the whistling of an ambulance that day when Lin left me for the last time. He embraced me once more in the snow and sent me to school. I went to bed and woke up by the sharp whistling of an ambulance. My heart forgot to beat, for suddenly I heard a voice, telling me that Lin's love for me was ending. I've fought bravely to keep his love. Where is he now? Do I have to give him up? I made a resolution last Mid-autumn Festival. Will it come true? It's blowing so hard now. I hear falling leaves weeping in the cold air.

September 6

I've just finished *Moment in Peking*. I am dragged back to the 1930s and hate the Japanese as much as Mulan did when her best friend was raped and her families were killed by the invading Japanese. I wonder why the Japanese were so cruel and barbarous. Didn't they have hearts, red and warm hearts that can feel and love? I know sometimes we have to forgive in order to live in peace but there must be justice. If humans can not correct themselves then God has to do it. Time can heal any pain but when a nation was treated brutally and unfairly, there must be a deep wound in God' heart that can't be healed. The Chinese ancestors asked us to be always "harmonious". Confucius folded his hands gently together and emphasized the "goodness" and "benevolence" of the world while smiling to his obedient countrymen. If God had seen this ancient and feminine nation, he would surely have said: You are the son I love. I believe in God. I believe in love. I believe in the innocence of my people. So that's why I am so confused at Japan's beastly massacre. Why did they do it? Why won't they apologize?

September 7

I've caught a cold and hope I can recover quickly. Six has decided to give up her dream of doing postgraduate work. Her family is too poor. She has to work as soon as possible. No one has encouraged her to further her study except me. She has bought some books enthusiastically but has to give up in the end. She felt very sorry about it. I tried to comfort her while she was crying under her quilt. Well, there are so many ways to live and live happily. When we can't afford a dream we have to give it up. There is nothing we can do about it. I still hold fast to this graduate dream though not as firmly as usual. Maybe I am not well. I have a running nose and cough a lot. But deep inside I know something is missing. I am not a complete person any more. My inner strength is losing. I would read and write and run to the library as everyone else but I can't help wondering the point of doing all these things. Life will be over one way or another. Why try so hard? What's the use of being earnest when no one is serious about you? I am shocked by such decadent thought. Lin has changed me. He lifted me up to heaven and then threw me down to hell. I've tried not to think this way. I choose not to lose trust in him for I can't afford to lose trust in myself.

September 9

Harvey asked me out this afternoon. While we were standing by the bank a little boy came up to sell his withered roses to Harvey. No, we don't want roses. Harvey was too gentle to refuse a little cheeky boy. So we decided to walk away from him but the flower boy followed us, trying to put his hand into Harvey's pocket. I turned and shouted at him, "Get away you little pigtail!" He was frightened and ran away while warning Harvey, "Your wife is a wicked girl!" Harvey laughed while I pretended to chase this little devil. He ran faster and faster, his little pigtail floating in the air. Now when I thought of it I felt ashamed. His family must be very poor. When other children are having education in school, he comes to sell withered flowers. I shouldn't have shouted at him.

September 11

I'm afraid I've become a fatalist for no matter how I try there is always something I can't get. I've tried to be good, patient, understandable and sensible, but my only hope of seeing Lin once more refuses to come true. After a long time of depression I feel hatefully relieved now, believing that all things are prearranged by destiny. What can we do about our destiny? Very little! So I won't be extremely discouraged if I can't get what I want. Is it cynical? Well, life is after all a play. We shouldn't be too serious with it.

O my God, I saw him! His big black eyes flashed in my direction when I walked to the toilet. Lin was back! He was playing a joke on me! I rushed to him only to find he was NOT Lin but someone who resembled Lin so much. The boy looked straight into my eyes and asked what the matter was. What was the matter? Why weren't you Lin? I stood before this fake Lin, flushing like a budding little girl. He thought I was out of my mind and walked into his classroom without a word. I tried to look for him after class but he was gone. Was it an illusion? Did I really see Lin, or a fake Lin? O, the world would be so beautiful if only there was love that can be touched and felt. The Mid-autumn Festival is coming. Will my resolution made last year come true? Will Lin come to see me on the reunion day?

September 11

The day is wonderful. I feel so comfortable to hang around with girls and share their innocent pleasure on finding a little purse after walking three blocks in a crowded city. I don't lead any more. I am too tired of being a leader. I follow the mainstream and make peace with my surprised roommates and the world.

September 13

The moon is almost full tonight. If life is a stage, thank God for every episode that has made my life worth playing. Bless my love for me. Lin, are you enjoying the moon?

September 14

I still cough a lot. I'm afraid the divine happiness I create for myself will be broken once the round moon is gone. Life is absolute and unconditional. I could wish good wishes but can't make all come true. I am quite clear of this rule so I am calm, contented and happy with only a hope. One has to make life easier to live by making concessions.

The feeling, that what I want desperately is coming, makes me happy and brave. Lin is on my mind every day, every hour, every minute. I really miss Lin. I see him everywhere so I smile in all directions and even giggle in my dream. My roommates are worried that I am mad due to the high fever. What am I looking for in a man? There are so many handsome guys in the world. Why am I so attached to Lin? A life without him is like a life without a purpose or breath. I miss him and I am sure he misses me too. God, please bless this divine love. Please let me have a dream and be happy with my imagination.

September 18

I walked slowly in the rose garden after lunch. I noticed a lonely girl sitting on the ground. She looked so out of place that I pitied her immediately. I tried to smile to her but she was too shy to look up. So I left her alone to study her toe while I went to talk with the fragrant China roses. A China rose is like a rose when in bud but changes to a hot peony when blooms. What is Lin doing now? The more I think of him the more I have confidence in his goodness.

September 20

The whole class went to attend a lecture on international relations this afternoon. It was held in a magnificent hall which made us feel very important for the first time in the college life.

Six was too embarrassed to eat her sunflower seeds in such a hall. She stared at the old man on the platform seriously and bent down to take notes. After the lecture I asked her how she felt about the lecture. She said the carpet was so soft and the hall so elegant that she did not concentrate on the lecture at all.

September 21

The prospectus from the Foreign Affairs College has come. I read the old examination papers and a thunder cracked over my head. The Japanese paper makes no sense to me at all. The translation paper is more discouraging. It contains large paragraphs of old Chinese essays from Confucius' *Analects*. I must come to the core quickly. Don't read idle novels. Don't complain about political theories any more. I need to be practical and efficient.

September 24

It's raining so hard. I lie in bed, not knowing what I would do once I get up. I am strangely upset. Suddenly I think of Franklin's famous sentence on marriage and eyes. Well even with two eyes open one still couldn't see clearly what love is. After marriage one can see clearly even with one eye open since all the fancies about love have to come down to reality. There are so many things not as beautiful as we expect. Love is a divine dream. Once you wake up, the splendid aura surrounding love will fade away. To live we have to find some pieces of the broken dream in everyday life. And we are sure to find some since human kind has to go on dreaming and living. I find my precious piece and get up to read *Analects* in the garden.

September 25

Love exists when we can't get it. It lifts us to ecstasy, pushes us down to despair and then drives us to hell. Maybe something is dying in my heart. When a seed refuses to sprout after painstaking care, there must be something wrong from the very beginning. I begin to know what it means by one's heart crying. When I wash my face, hot tears would rush down into the basin; when I eat, suddenly I lose my appetite; when I read, I would stare blankly at the page and when night comes, I go to bed without saying good night to my roommates. God, I am so sad deep inside.

September 26

Somebody wrote an open letter to the leaders of the department, complaining against our new foreign teacher Miriam. Many students signed their stupid names. I was agitated and refused to sign my name when the letter was passed on to me. Miriam was such a nice lady. Why did they do this nasty thing to her? She had only given us one lecture. How can they judge her so irrationally? She was a different lady from the Americans. She treated us like equal adults who had independent thought. I love her style and begin to like Canada. Maybe someday I can visit that vast land and her mild people.

September 27

Don't know why my heart is shrinking tighter and tighter. The phone can work now but what's the point of it? The number has changed. Lin can't find me even if he wants. The only pleasure is snatched away from me. I feel empty. The inner strength is fading away. What will happen to me? Why am I so painful? Why am I so miserable, sad and restless?

September 29

My dear friend Pretty will get married on October 3. I will go to attend her wedding in our hometown. I will lose my dear friend to marriage. I don't know whether I can handle it well.

I wrote a letter to Lin to tell him my new phone number. I am even sick of thinking of him now. He is too vague and remote to my dying expectations. I can be happy without remembering him for a little while. Sometimes I am quite comfortable with Harvey. Maybe I should abandon Lin. There is still much fun and wonder for me to explore. I need to be happy and I will be.

The party before our teaching building sounds so exhilarating. I close the book and go down to join the happy creatures.

October 1

The National Day!

Happy birthday my dear country! It's raining so hard.

A notion popped up when I was thinking of Lin. I shouldn't hate him secretly. I remember he told me once that he worked in a construction team and slept in the open field in cold winter. He is trying to change his destiny. He is independent and brave. I should be proud of him instead of complaining about his negligence. I shouldn't be selfish. He would surely be unhappy if he fails to make a fortune from his hard work. Yet his happiness is what I want. No one can have a sense of security if one's value can't be accepted by the society. To realize one's social value is a long and hard process during which a determined man has to neglect something. I should respect and encourage him. Thank my heart for this discovery. I shouldn't curse him at all. I should walk out of that narrow-minded and emotional little girl. I have promised to understand him then I must think for him instead of myself. I feel relieved now. I feel strong again.

Harvey is also growing. He sounded like a real man when he thundered, "Go! Go to prepare for the exams!" He forced me to go to study when I couldn't tear away from him after squandering the whole afternoon with him in the park. He sincerely hopes that I can pass the exams and be a diplomat. He has only me in his heart, no one else, not even himself. I don't know how to pass the four college years without Harvey. Even if I don't marry him later on, he would still be the most important one in my college memory.

October 2

I fell asleep on the train and woke up right on time. Pretty sent a boy to pick me up at the railway station. I am with my dear Pretty at her brother's home now. We've just had a bath at a public bathroom. The little bride was not as mysterious as I thought. Her brother has already gone to the old village to prepare for the wedding tomorrow. We share a room with her sister-in-law. The room is quiet, too quiet for the last night of a single Pretty. She would be a bride tomorrow. She would be someone's wife. Why do people want to get married? I hope tomorrow a successful day. The little bride is sitting beside me now, trying to find a right train for me to take so that I can go back to school without missing her wedding.

October 3

Is it a wedding? Well, it looks more like a big gathering for the country fellows. The small yard of Pretty's grandparents sees many old people in shabby and traditional clothes. They are cooks, assistants, and guests. They are all kinsmen or some close friends of her good-natured grandparents. They all look content and happy. The little bride is sitting on the bed, trying her new red dress and red shoes. She eats little. The helping villagers are enjoying themselves. An old granny pulls and pushes the wind bellow in the warm sun. When streams come out of the big pot, she yells at another old woman who empties a basket of jiaozi in the hot water. Soon jiaozi is ready. An old grandpa comes with a dozen of bowls and scoops the jiaozi into the bowls which are delivered to the guests from other villages by another helping hand. They are so happy with food, old friends, laughter and sunshine. I don't think they know who is getting married today.

It's about half past ten. The bridegroom has not come. Pretty is a little anxious. She asks me to accompany her to the toilet. I stand outside of the simple toilet to be her guard while she relieves herself quickly in the open air. Afterwards I escort my beautiful Pretty to her bride chamber again. She sits quietly on the bed while the helping kinsmen come now and then to fetch steamed bread or fried dough in the wooden box in her room. Actually this is her mother's room and all the food for the wedding is kept here. So she has no privacy in the last hours of her girlhood. I walk out to see whether the groom has arrived or not. This is a backward village. The lanes are muddy and dirty. Old fashioned clothes can be seen everywhere. Little children look strangely dull and silly. They would stare at me as if I were from outer space. There is no smile on their expressionless faces. I smile at a little girl who has a running nose. She hides behind her mother shyly. I feel sorry for these poor children. They may become as smart and lively as city children if only their families could afford proper education for them. However, only a few portions of the countryside children can get good education and fewer can get a proper high school education. Most of these innocent souls would never leave this land or have the chance to see the colorful and advanced world outside their backward hometown. I feel so sad. They are Clinton, Harvey, Pretty, Ben, Rui and Patricia. We looked as hopeless as them ten years ago but we are different now. We have squeezed into the tight- closed doors of colleges and are working for a future. Will this generation come out of poverty? Will they have the chance to be what they want to be? What can we do for them? I feel so anxious to go back to school. I am eager to study. Why hasn't the groom come?

Will I get married? When? How? Whom?

Suddenly comes the loud sound of " 唢呐 "(suo na)—a very Chinese musical instrument. With one breath of the trumpet it can blow you to tears of great joy and unbearable sadness. It means marriage and burial. I have been to lots of funerals dry-eyed, but when 唢呐 pierces the air with such extreme sadness I can't help weeping for the dead and the alive. I weep for the dead because they cease to exist. No matter what I can never see them again. A play is over and the curtain is drawn forever. I weep for the alive because what a miserable life they are living. Year in year out I watch them struggle against poverty, disasters, illness and humiliation. I follow the coffin in the wild field with people in white. They are a part of this barren land. They spread seeds, hew weeds, get in the crops and then bury themselves into the earth. The trumpets would blow their 唢呐 into the air when the coffin is thrown into the hole. Then helping hands will shovel some dirt onto the wooden coffin and forever the dead is gone. However, the 唢呐 I hear now is heralding the happiest moment of a Chinese. It's strange that we use the same musical instrument for funeral and marriage. Well, maybe we are right. With marriages boys and girls are accepted into the social world as men and women. They are going to spread seeds, hew weeds, get in the crops and then bury themselves in the earth. We only use the loudest sound at these two occasions. When a sound goes to extremes, it becomes a defiant, a struggle and a tragedy. The bridegroom comes for his beautiful bride in the loud noise. He is a schoolmate in senior high school. Pretty and he have been close friends since then. I am really happy for their love. But, alas, tears rush down when Pretty comes out into the warm sun.

She smiles to the old villagers, many of whom are wiping their eyes. She smiles at her husband who is sweating and nervous. She winks at me before I can dry my tear-stricken face. She is as fresh as the morning dew. How I want to give her a big hug and a gentle kiss! No, I can't. I am a Chinese.

Then she is carried on the rented car. According to the tradition Pretty should not come out and onto the car so quickly. She should wait in her chamber till her husband gives her 100 Yuan while 唢呐 blows the loudest sound and the fireworks cracks the happiest noise. However, time has changed. She loves him too much to let him sweat nervously in public. So she comes out when she sees him through the window. Many old classmates have come to celebrate the big occasion. We urge her husband Chun to pick Pretty up in his arms and enter the car together. Then goes the car to his home in another village. There are seven more cars to take the relatives. I am in one of those. Pretty insists that I should take the car next to hers so that I can be close to her. It takes a long time to get out of Pretty's muddy village. Some neighbors are burning a fire in front of their gates. Some villagers block the cars with tree trunks. These are the rules of this old village. The first one is to wish the little bride good luck at the new home and the latter one asks the groom's family for money since they are taking this village's girl away. Then there are endless fireworks and cannons " bee-bee-bo-bo!"" Dong----ka!" The sun is hot above when we finally get into Chun's home in an apple orchard. His parents and relatives are kind. They receive Pretty joyfully and hide her in the newly decorated room. Many farmers, old and young, squeeze in to see the beautiful bride who is in a white gown. Her mother-in-law closes the door and suggests that Pretty should have a little rest. After a while she is asked to change into the traditional dress---a red Qipao. "Der-----wa!" Suona pierces everyone's heart and pushes the atmosphere in the apple orchard to the peak. As custom goes, Pretty eats a roasted "Mo" (steamed bread) and a spring onion on the bed. Then we all go to a big restaurant in town for a formal lunch. I see many old faces there including Mr. Zhang who taught us math in high school and who made me cry hysterically one day with his cold remarks about a "stupid girl who knew nothing about math". Well, let bygones be bygones. I greet him dutifully as a student. Confucius told us: once your teacher, always your father. While we are having a table of special dishes Pretty comes to us with her husband. She smiles and thanks us for our coming. Her two dimples are deep and laughing. She is happy. So I am happy too. Before she leaves she pressed a fifty note in my hand. I tried to protest, but she said she would cry if I did not accept it. She doesn't forget my poor situation even on her wedding day. How I want to be close to her the whole day but I have to take the train to Zhengzhou in the late afternoon. Pretty was still making toasts table after table when I took my leave. I wish God would always bless Pretty and her dear husband.

I am on the train now. After six hours' standing in the crowded train I come back to school on time. I wash my face, lie on my little bed and the light goes off.

October 9

I am learning charcoal drawing now. I drew my first eye last night. My roommates encouraged me by saying that it looked so real.

October 11

It's raining hard. I don't have an umbrella. How can I go to another college for the painting class? Well, I have to make it anyway.

I came back on time for Miriam's video class. She is showing us a Canadian concert now. The western people look so easy-going and happy. They move with the music and applaud so genuinely for every performer. Maybe I can dance and scream in a western country too. Chinese people are too stable and calm. The remote and heavy air of this ancient "middle kingdom" does not encourage such personal outrage. What is freedom? Someday I need to go abroad to be another Patricia.

October 13

For a time I don't know what to do next. No, it is not true. I know there are lots of book to read but my enthusiasm just refuses to be aroused. I sit idly in the classroom when everyone else has gone for lunch. My only consolation now comes from my charcoal drawing. Maybe there will be a miracle at the end of this session class.

I've finished the second reading of *Mao Zedong's thought*. What is this man of Mao Zedong? I begin to really admire him. I love his writing style—short, sharp and powerful.

The painting teacher is trying to make a living by asking us for extra money. I don't hate him. I pity him. If I could become somebody one day, I would set up a big saloon where everything is free for artists. They are a special class who have a noble heart, but still they can't live on wind and water.

October 14

It's sunny today. I love the warm day in late autumn. On the way to the classroom I picked up a fallen parasol leaf. It was melancholy red with a light yellow margin. It was beautiful. I stuck it on the back wall of the classroom. Many classmates wondered where I found such a perfect leaf. Actually we see the leaves every day. We walk by them, tramp on them but are seldom inspired by their beauty. However, when they are presented to us as an individual they catch our eyes. So collectivism is not always right. If everyone can try to be oneself and doesn't lose oneself in a muddled sea of crowds, there would be many more innovations and much more fun.

October 18

Good morning, Pearl!

Today is Wednesday. We're having Canadian Culture by Miriam. Surprisingly, everyone seems in high spirit. I see smiles on the faces which looked so cruel when they conspired against Miriam.

October 20

Eva, Miriam, I and an American teacher Susan went to the city museum this afternoon. Susan bought a pack of gums at a stand and shared with us. When the woman asked her how much she earned in the university, she answered clearly in Chinese: " 这是我的隐私 !" which means " mind your own business!". My dear Chinese woman smiled shyly at such a rude answer. Eva and I felt too embarrassed to chew the gum. We walked across the city square and marched to the museum, while Miriam helped to keep the conversation going. Suddenly Susan stopped. She put her bag between her legs and started taking off the sweater on the street and then tied it around her neck. She did it so naturally in the central part of China where foreigners were still stared at like bizarre animals. She took no notice of the staring looks and walked on defiantly. At last we were in the museum. An assistant came up happily as if his gloomy day was broken up with the coming of two women from outer space. He followed us around and kept asking where the two ladies came from. He followed us to the ancient bronze hall, the old china hall and the fossils hall. Susan's eyebrows were knotted. I whispered to the man to leave us alone quickly in case he would be ridiculed as if "all Chinese bother people like tiresome bugs". Two hours later we walked out of the museum. Miriam and Susan said they had a nice time. Well, really? Eva looked at me with puzzled eyes. How could they have a good time when the harmonious air was wounded again and again? On the way back we came across a building. Miriam wondered who lived in the building. I said maybe it was a power plant, for the gate was black as if trucks and trucks of coal had scratched on it. Susan was not satisfied with such a "fuzzy" answer. She walked across the street in the heavy traffic furiously and came back to say that it was not a power plant. She was not sure what it was, but it was NOT a power plant. How touched I was at the westerner's pursuit for truth! Pooh! I began to miss the easy and comfortable air with my roommates who did not have such a strong "scientific spirit".

October 21

It's drizzling now. Harvey invited me out. He was excited and happy like a rash boy. I was happy too but did not know what to say to him. I felt so right to be with him. College life would be incomplete without him. No matter what happens in the future I hope he can be happy and lucky, with me or without me.

I called my second sister. My nephew had long forgotten the fight with me last vacation.

He was too spoiled to be my favorite boy. When I couldn't stand his mischievous ways, I slapped his face and sent him crying and screaming. My sister was horrified. I felt so bad afterwards. I went to wander in the storm, hating myself and the hard situation. Why couldn't I be patient? My sister took me from the hell of home and treated me so well. Why did I slap her only son? While I was furious at myself I heard my nephew's voice. He came out looking for me with an umbrella. His big eyes flashed timidly in the darkness. My sister told me that he stopped crying when I banged the door behind me and ran into the storm. He was afraid that I went home. He liked me too much to let me go. So he took an umbrella and came out to look for me. Hot tears rushed out when I heard his na?ve voice calling me "Little auntie! Little auntie!" I was so ashamed. Then I bought him a toy bear with my pocket money the next day. He had long forgotten the slap, hadn't he? He asked his dear little auntie to buy him a plane. I said yes of course. How I wish to take him to a plane trip one day!

The night is gentle and peaceful. I should have enjoyed myself if my mind could stop working for a little while. No, it doesn't. It has been moving faster and faster with dreams, boys, exams, love, excitement and fear.

October 27

I thought of my second little niece Yuan when I was still lying in bed. She is so piteous, neglected by the two queens at home----her mother and her grandmother. No one took her to see a doctor when her hands were frozen and her little face twisted with pain and coldness. How cruel was I! I tried to turn the harsh situation for her at home. I named her as my favorite. I took her in my arms when her big sister tried to pinch her. I let her sit by me while I was blowing the wind bellows. However, didn't I scream at her when she wailed loud? Didn't I cut her with cold eyes when she wetted my bed? Didn't I yell at her and let her go to hell when she disobeyed me from time to time? I was such a horrible aunt. I am afraid of thinking of her. Her always tear-stricken face and frozen hands work as a sharp knife, cutting my conscience and heart. She is such a passionate and kind-hearted girl though she is treated like an underdog at home. She was the only one to jump with joy when my father came back from selling bean curd village after village. She was the only one who cried when I had to leave for school. She would follow her mother around like a faithful little guide if the latter did not push her aside impatiently. She would empty her grandma's urine pot if the latter would give her a tiny smile. Poor darling, why did you come to this hostile world? You came when your parents were trying so hard to bear a male heir for the Liu family in the wildness. You came to suffer hunger and indifference. You came to torture my weak heart and unsteady conscience. The most dreadful thing for me is to suddenly think of Yuan when I am trying to sleep. I cry under the quilt for the many wrongs I and the families have done to her. She is such a special child. I even admire her calmness before strangers and her little wisdom of serving herself with the meals so neatly when she was still a toddler. I admire her for her brave protest to any pressure. She would say "go to hell!" when someone shouts at her. She would pinch a dog if it dares to snarl at her. Yet, she never uses a harsh word to me. She would weep piteously when I shout at her. I asked her once why she cried. She said she was afraid that little auntie wouldn't love her any more. I hugged her and told her she was always and always my little darling. O, what a little baby!

It's getting colder and colder now. I must write home to warn the family about Yuan's hands. They mustn't get frozen this year. It makes me feel good to do something for this poor, smart and delicate child who is now only three years old.

October 28

Yingzi called me this noon. She asked me to accommodate her boyfriend Mr. Wu for some days. She met him while she was involved in a marketing scam and was cheated of all her 5,000 Yuan. He helped her out of that black money-sucking hole and they fell in love. She took him home but her parents did not like this southerner from Sichuan province. They forbade her to keep the relationship with him. She asked me to find a room for him and she would come to meet him when she helped harvest all the apples in her parents' orchard. Then they would go to Canton together and be "farmer workers". I agreed to help them. I called Harvey. He was willing to share his bed with Mr. Wu. It made me happy to see true love and to be of any help to this pair of separated "mandarin ducks".

October 31

What's wrong today? I can't believe it! I only have 100 Yuan in my bank card. That bank clerk was impatient to deal with a poor client. He smacked his thin lips, narrowed his long eyes and showed me to the door. I hate him. I hope China can join in the WTO quickly so that advanced foreign banking system can compete with the domestic ones. Competition is good.

I have to borrow some money to enroll for the postgraduate exam. Why is it always so hard for me? Money! Money! Where can I borrow some money for Yingzi's boyfriend? He is penniless now. What shall I do? I don't know. This is how things go. I can do nothing to change it. I'll study hard. I must succeed in the exam. I shall never go hungry when I can work after graduation. Be calm, Pearl.

Yingzi finally came to meet her boy in the afternoon. He was overjoyed at his angel. He was transfixed to a lively and talkative boy though he had caught a cold. Yingzi laughed a lot and aloud. They were genuinely happy, so happy that I envied them. Yingzi shared my bed for the last night before she would elope with him to the south.

November 1

After a simple breakfast I saw Yingzi off at the north gate of Zhengzhou University this morning. The sun was just rising. Mr. Wu was still coughing which made their elopement covered with a dash of tragedy. Yingzi was determined and happy. She swung their heavy bundle over her shoulder and said goodbye to a tearful me. My dear Yingzi who was my accountant and bought my meals in high school was leaving for another city. God, bless her and her boy.

Harvey borrowed some money for me. I was touched. He regarded me as part of himself. Thank God for sending someone to take care of me. Thanks. No matter what happens Harvey would always be my dearest boy. Thanks.

November 5

Wherever I go I take a simple room in my heart. It is where Lin and I shared so many nights together. It is where Lin boiled me eggs and spread a table of dishes to welcome me. It is where

Lin held me tightly in his hungry arms and whispered how much he missed me. I take it with me. It is the origin of my love and pain. I spent the happiest and truest time there with Lin. How things have changed! Yet something will last forever.

November 7

I was standing on the balcony of the teaching building when the strong wind began to whistle far and near. It was howling, roaring, crying and fighting its way into the classroom through every crack. I opened my arms to welcome the awesome breath of heaven. How I wish to fly away in the strong wind!

November 8

I woke up to find a white world. Snow has covered everything with a white veil quietly during the night. It is still dancing gently in the air. Oh, how can God create such delicate, sweet, and beautiful creatures! I walk in the fresh air to say goodbye to autumn. Three days ago I was lying on the dry grass with Harvey by the bank and now snow has covered it with white quilt. Only yesterday did I linger by the old parasol tree and kissed its falling leaves, now they are buried in snow. Winter is here to replace autumn. Dear you, do you believe the changes of seasons? Of course you do. What a silly question! Yet do you have this strong and clear sensation as I do now? I heard the last breath of autumn and felt its reluctant pulse. When the first snow of winter comes, my heart is filled with sincere thanks and genuine pity for the coming and leaving. Farewell, dear sad autumn. Welcome you, flying winter. Nature is so pure and so absolute.

I thought of the winter days I spent with Lin. I was so happy then, the happiest girl of the 20th century. Lin loves snow. Where is he now? How is he? Is he cold? I still remember the short and hard pads in his shoes. He was so anxious about his work even in the cold snowing morning. We shared the last breakfast and he walked me to school. The soberness and seriousness on his face have been engraved in my mind since he turned to walk away.

Harvey called last night to remind me to put on more clothes. I know I am cared for. He is mine. Harvey needs a heavy coat and a pair of warm shoes this winter. I must save some money to buy my boy the necessary for winter.

November 9

It's still bitingly cold today. We are going to have Miriam's class on Canadian Culture. She asked us to prepare a debate on the Quebec question. Should it leave or must it stay? I think it should stay to be a part of the country. I hate parting. Every parting inflicts pain and sorrow on everyone concerned. Be united and work it out if there are any grievances.

November 10

I keep worrying about the enrollment forms I filled in for the postgraduate exam. Did I write my name wrong? Did I give them my correct address? Did I choose the right major? Did I write neatly enough? What's wrong with me? I am so excited and nervous. As soon as I handed in the form something precious and heavy was taken away from my chest. I am not as enthusiastic and confident as I was before the final enrollment. This is not right. I need to be sure of myself. Be calm, Pearl.

English novels are necessary to keep me thinking and feeling in a different world. I've tried to keep myself away from novels. It's wrong. Why can't I read the books that can restore a period of history to me? The beautiful sentences and thoughts can lift me up to another level.

November 11

Fine day.

I have to be serious with "Political Theories". I seem to know everything but my mind goes blank when I read the old exam papers.

It's 3 p.m. now. At 6 p.m. Six, Miriam and I will go to have spicy rice noodle at a small village near our campus. I hope for a good time together. I feel a little dizzy. Pray it won't be a cold.

Yes, we three had a marvelous time. Miriam enjoyed the spicy noodle and then invited Six and me to have beer in her apartment. She was so natural and kind. Six told Miriam about my love with Lin. The beer gave her courage and sharp words. She called me a fool and begged Miriam to wake me up from this stupid dream. Miriam looked at me with great interest and sympathy. The beer was warming up in my brain, too. I preached my grand love philosophy to them no matter how tightly Six covered her ears with her fat hands. I murmured at first, then talked hotly when Six retorted back and then screamed when she pouted her lips defiantly. Good Miriam helped me. She comforted me by saying that "Follow your heart, Patricia. Your heart is engaged to this man".

Thank Miriam for the night. Thank Six for her genuine concern about my mental health. I feel uncomfortable all over. I am afraid I've caught a cold. We talked about Lin tonight. Miriam does not know how much she has helped me during these lonely days. She is so good-natured and understanding. I see great sympathy in her grey eyes. It is sympathy for all suffering creatures. She understands my helpless love for Lin. She encourages me to be myself. I told her I had trust in Lin. Yes, I do, for the memories are beautiful, moving and true. If I'm still in a dream, so what, I refuse to wake up. As long as I still trust him, I will feel happy. As long as I still love him I will have the energy to move on, though the love is not as carefree and naive as it was. I know he cares for me. May God take care of him!

My brain refuses to entertain more nonsense. So, good night, the world!

November 12

Somebody may work to death. That is because work is not a pleasure for them. Today is rather an ugly day for me. I felt bad and gave Harvey a cold shoulder when we went shopping together. No one can interest me. There is nothing to work for. Life is such a burden. I felt sick at the dirty northerners walking on the dirty street of a dirty city while I was squeezing into a dirty and crowded trolley. I was in a terrible mood. There was no strength left in my shaky body. I quarreled with Harvey and went back to sleep. Maybe I need to be patient with life. I have to and must live it peacefully if not happily. It was my intention to be nasty to Harvey. I always lose control in a swirling crowd. Among all the boys and girls Harvey cares about me most. Though his love is still at a sentimental level, he is trying to love me as an adult does. I shouldn't be nasty to him. I must make up with him. I feel the pain myself if I hurt someone who doesn't deserve it.

Thank God for another passing day. Take care of me, God; I am so alone.

November 14

I called Harvey after supper. I was so sweet over the phone that he came to have a walk with me by the bank. Then I complained about my sensitive nerves and slight headache while he was enchanted by my childish way. Then I sighed and leaned against his shoulder. Harvey, do you think it will be better for my health and my study if we can rent a room out of the campus? I asked him shyly. A long pause. He did not comprehend. What? Live together out of campus? No, we are still students! Unmarried boys and girls shouldn't live together! He looked at me curiously as if I was a slut. I felt so ashamed in front of Harvey the SAGE. Shit! Unmarried boys and girls can have sex in the park, in classrooms or wherever is dark. Why can't they live together? What's the difference? I was furious. How dare Harvey refuse my plan? He should jump with joy and hug me instead of accusing me of breaking college rules. Pooh, rules be hanged! I said coldly,

"You are a dead log" and ran back to the classroom where Miriam was showing the class another VCD. It was a concert by several bands. There were half nudities, smoking guys and strange things in it. My head spun at the exploding music from heavy metals, bald singers, stupid sex and endless yelling......What's wrong with them? Or what's wrong with me?

November 17

Harvey called last night to say that he agreed to my plan of renting a room out of the campus. It's a fine day today. I'll go to look for a suitable room. I dreamt Lin last night. I hated him in my dream.

Chrysanthemums are blooming now. I pick a yellow one and put it in an empty bottle. Sometimes we need only a little whim to light up our days. I'll match the yellow chrysanthemum with green leaves tomorrow. Thank God for the beautiful world.

November 18

Harvey said I should let him go if I couldn't afford to love him anymore. This outrageous remark was caused by my contemptuous reaction when he came to me, still in that shabby jacket which was too small for him. I had warned him not to wear it any more. He looked ridiculous in it and I didn't want to hold hands with a ridiculous boy. Yet, there he came, with that particularly tiny old jacket on. I held my head high and suggested he throw his jacket into a trashcan nearby. He was nervous and anxious to please me at first but retorted back when I compared him with Lin. He said, "If you can't love me anymore, leave me alone. Don't despise my love for you. It is as pure as lily. You are a bad girl. You don't deserve it anymore." Thus said he left me by the bank. I wanted to cry but my eyes were dry. I stood there dumbfounded. Am I abandoned by Harvey? Harvey has abandoned me? How weird! He is my own flesh. How dare he be so ironical and threatening? I was almost afraid of him for some moments. Maybe I will go back to the state when I can't talk due to my confused mind. But one thing has been made definitely clear to me----the base on which I nurture a love for Lin is loose and gone. I have depended on Harvey's total care and unconditional love too long to leave him alone. He is like a part of me now. I can curse him, pinch him, make fun of him but can't afford to lose him. Yet, love is a bargain. I can't afford his love anymore. I compare Harvey with Lin all the time and treat Harvey unfairly. I've made myself a fool. Harvey is after all not a home nor a family. He is also a stranger. He needs to be paid for his care for me. I can't pay him back in the way he deserves. Sorry, boy. Thanks are really too cheap for his love. Meek Harvey can frighten me because I am so guilty inside. I've nothing to say now. I'll feel terribly lonely if Harvey deserts me, but I'll be terribly wrong if I ask more than I can pay. Somebody said knowledge is power. Well, it depends. I've read almost all the books in the library. Why am I still so weak? I think and think but can't find the right answer. God, forgive me. I am so sinful.

November 21

I feel really bad now. Blue curtains by my seat are whirling in the wind. They wrap me up, slash my face and wave back. I feel like dying and vomit some bitter water. I am a little scared. What's wrong?

November 24

I've thought of studying in a quiet room for a long time but every time I think of leaving my dear roommates tears would sting my eyes. Why do I love them so much though they have hurt me now and then? We have been hard enemies, competitors for scholarships, rivals for some stupid boys, yet there is something true and mysterious in Room 202 where tears are bitter and laughter are genuine. How can I leave them during the last days of college life? Yet, I'm having a hard time to concentrate in the tiny classroom where my classmates are all studying as if there were no tomorrow. I feel nervous in such a tense atmosphere. I need to relax and enjoy myself. God, what shall I do? You're pushing me to a direction. Where will it lead?

November 25

I keep imagining "that room of mine". Some mysterious power is pushing me to that direction. Ok, go and find a room! I called Harvey and we wandered near and far to look for a rented room. I was a little ashamed when fat landladies watched us with "that" in their cynical eyes. I would have given up if Harvey wasn't there holding my hand. At last my room showed itself behind top tree branches. We sat in the empty room shyly and hugged. Then we went to buy curtains, bed sheets, and desk lamp in the cheapest market. We were making a "home". Harvey was happy. He stood on a stool and set up the green curtain to the only window. He made the bed, and swept the cement floor while I was sticking some parasol leaves on the wall. The only purpose of my renting a room should be the study for the postgraduate exam. My days here should be planned.

Lin, I am honest to you. Please understand me and forgive me. No one can ever take your special place in my heart. Yet, I'll try to leave you alone. I must face the near reality.

God, thank you for taking care of me!

November 26

Now I believe in Freud's theories on sex. I feel great today though a little tired physically. Harvey was tender and caring though he was not as passionate and delicious as Lin. I even hated God for pushing me into such a dilemma between spiritual longing and carnal desire. Harvey attacked the very important front that I had preserved for Lin for more than 10 months. Something in my heart cracked when Harvey held me affectionately in his arms under the quilt.

When I went out of the library just now I looked in the direction where Harvey might be having a class. Harvey has always been kind to me. I've taken his love for granted so long. Am I starting to love him? God punish me!

Good night!

November 27

Maybe I've caught a cold. I feel sleepy and extremely tired. I borrowed the "Four Books" yesterday—*the Great Learning, the Mean, the Analects* and *Mencius*. The four classical and philosophical books have exerted such great power over me through their simple languages. I become quiet and benign once I smell the ancient scent from the yellow paper. Be obedient! Be filial! Be kind! Be friendly! Be faithful! Be innocent! Take the middle way! Never go to extremes! Well, I wonder how my dear ancestors ever made their living by being so docile. How can they be expected to defend their "middle kingdom" and "their heavenly prince" from the barbarian invasion of ferocious species who were taller, stronger, prouder, more scientific, more realistic and more aggressive? Their philosophy on harmony is not wrong but it is pulling my legs when I have to fight my way in this secular world. So I put aside the four books and opened Zhuangzi. He is worshipped as the father of Chinese Taoism. His wild imagination, splendid languages and elusive laughs at life lifted him high above the ordinary people. I read his dreams of butterflies and drifted into sleep. I followed the huge butterfly over a brook, across a large piece of grassland and perched on a blooming rose. Was I following a butterfly or was I a butterfly? I woke up and lost myself in the warm sun.

November 30

Harvey is going to take the National English Test for non-English majors soon. I must help him. It's said that if they can't pass the exam they won't be able to have the bachelor's degree at the graduation. Harvey complained that he did not like English at all. Well, like it or not, he has to prepare for the exam. Even if the rule is stupid, we have to play along.

I went to the public shower room with Six this afternoon. After one hour's waiting in the rain we rushed in. She went to secure two taps while I fought my way to put our clothes into the lockers. Gosh, that was humiliating! Why couldn't the school build a bigger shower room? Taking a shower was like a nightmare. My heart was in my mouth 3 hours before the door was open and the fight for lockers and taps began. I should not have read so many Confucius books. What is the good of taking the middle way where other people are taking the shortest way? What is the good of being docile and peaceful when others are like hungry wolves? No good at all. I tried to "walk" into the bath room with dignity and pride. I took off my clothes at the normal speed and went to look for a tap. I wandered from this end to that end but couldn't find a free tap. I looked at hundreds of nudities and they looked at me. No one would let me share her tap or at least spray some hot water on my cold body. Confucius be hanged! This time I rushed in with Six, arm in arm. We pushed aside docile ones, stamped on aggressive ones and turned a deaf ear to screams and complaints. At last we won! We had two taps to our own. How relaxed were we in the hot water! There were nudities wandering from this end to that end. I smiled at them and asked them to share my tap. They stared at me and kept on wandering.

Another nightmare was waiting for us in the small lane

back to the dorm. There was always a man standing against the fence, his ugly penis trembling in the cold air. We had asked the doorkeeper to chase him away but he would come again to show his silly penis. The girls had to run quickly through the small lane after the shower. It was really annoying. I almost wanted to sting that ugly piece of meat with a sharp needle and send its owner to a sudden death. This was outrageous—a mad man taking advantages of girl students in the most prestigious university of this central province, AND no one did anything about it! I felt sick when we noticed that piece of meat again this afternoon. Its owner was like a dead black bat, clutching the fence tightly with two hands and his pants falling to his ankles. His eyes were looking far away like an idiot while that piece of meat was humiliating the passing girls. I was about to grab it and cut it to pieces when a policeman came and took the idiot away.

I told Harvey about this ugly thing. To my great surprise he laughed heartedly. Was it funny? No, it was disgusting! Later Harvey bought my dinner as a way of apology. The day ended well so the whole day was ok.

December 1

A new month has started. Life can be changed within a blink of eye. The last days of November were passed in a way out of my expectation. I was not sure, no, I was very sure that what I was doing with Harvey was not right. My heart was reluctant to respond. Something was agonizing. Well, I can't think of it now. This is life. We have to go on even when we don't have a clear idea about what is happening. I begin to like that room where Harvey is waiting for me. The gentle orange light from our little room was and is so appealing to me after a day's hard work in the classroom. Now I've almost woken up from the "oak boat" I made for myself after Lin's disappearance. What a change in the last days of college life! Time will prove whether it is right or wrong. Yet, now I'm afraid I need it as a little sign to show me that life can still go on when a heart is half dead. That little room has become a place of love which is desperate, risky and tearful.

I wish December a fulfilling month for all those who love me.

December 3

I'm glad that I am in the classroom instead of cuddling with Harvey in our "home". It's so hard to tear myself away from the warm little room and make my way to the classroom in the snow. Well, I did it. I am brave enough to go on with my dream crusade to be a diplomat.

I'll be very kind to Harvey so that the last days of college life should be sweet as sweet can be. Time will help me forget what I shouldn't remember.

Thank God for the chilly day!

December8

I should feel excited about love making but the fact was that there seemed to be a big void in my heart. I kept on thinking what the end of life would be while Harvey was busy with his triumphant adventure on my body. My mind was drifting to the very bottom of life to find that there was nothing which I really wanted because I did not know what I really needed. I lied to Harvey about many things but I was telling the truth when I told him I did not know what love was. I've been looking for it since I was a kid. Now I am 22 years old but I am still so confused or even more so. I felt indifferent and sad about what was going on with my body. I did it just to make Harvey happy as well as being a "bad girl" to do what was forbidden to do.

I went for a shower this afternoon. I looked at my body in the dripping water. Yes, there was a kind of beauty and arrogance in the milky skin and curved lines. Yet, how strange it was to me! It was cursing my wild ways and restless desire. I felt cheated. There was really nothing sweet, happy, noble, graceful and beautiful in putting two naked bodies together. A party was going on by the river when I came back from the public shower room. The words on the screen read: Song of Youth. Tears filled my eyes. Am I still a youth? Why do I feel so old? No, I am not old. I should never be old when I hold fast to my dreams.

December 9

Last night was a sweet nightmare. I was in despair this morning when I was too reluctant to get up while the unfulfilled dream was killing my conscience. Finally I forced myself up and shook hands with Harvey to say goodbye. I couldn't kiss him or hug him at that moment otherwise I would plunge into that great dilemma of life again. Falling in love is after all an ideal thing.

When you have to face the reality again after having traveled deep into each other's inner world, you may doubt whether life itself is wrong. The more love I make with Harvey the deeper I was lost in a vast sea of disappointment and emptiness as if my body and soul were penetrated by the continuous yet meaningless intercourse. I played a bad and bold girl last night for I couldn't find anything to cherish or keep as a secret. I wanted to see what was forbidden to me but found nothing.

When will be the time that there isn't such a clear-cut edge between dreams and realities? What am I looking for is less than love making or more than that? I will think about it later. There is only one month left before the postgraduate exam. I need to make a summary on Japanese and Politics; I need to do a systematic research on English; I need to learn some theories by heart. O, I should be armed to the teeth. God, thank you for all you've done for me. Bless me and all the people who love me.

Darkness is hovering down. My heart sinks when I remember I have to sleep in the room alone. I have asked Harvey to promise me that he won't come no matter how I beg him. I need to be sensible. I need to work hard instead of spending my precious time talking nonsense and making disappointing love. Be strong, Patricia. Think what you would do if you hadn't rented this room. I should make full use of the place instead of letting it be a burden to my study. Be cool and determined! Alas, what a coward was I! I was too scared to walk home alone. I stood on the deserted street for some time then dialed Harvey's BP. I did not want to feel so lonely in the cold winter evening.

December 10

What happened last night put some cold water to my frenzy mind. I was so disappointed at my own weakness of calling Harvey and also at his "nasty" ways of being what I despised as "coward" that I fell asleep very quickly. At dawn I was waken up by Harvey who was putting on his clothes very cautiously. He whispered that somebody was knocking at the door. I was frightened for a moment. Yes, footsteps, shouts, and heavy beating on the door! Gosh, what shall we do? No, we mustn't open the door. We are not married yet but we are living together. This is against the law. The policemen would take us away and put us in jail. No, we won't open the door. We shrunk into a corner of the bed while a torch light was searching the room through the window. Will they see us? I closed my eyes and held my breath while Harvey was gently weeping. We are not the only couple who are living together without a license. I heard loud shouts and heavy beating on other doors. Many wild mandarin ducks were scared out of their wits. Somehow it was funny. I laughed when the policemen finally left us alone. Harvey swore that he would never come here again. Well, good for him.

Tonight I will sleep in the dorm but I miss my room behind the winter branches. After all it is mine. Six and her boyfriend would be another pair of wild mandarin ducks tonight. Pray they wouldn't be bothered by the solemn beating of the LAW!

December 11

I heard from my sister. She was worried that I did not have

enough food so she mailed me 500 Yuan. I felt the warmth of home at her familiar handwriting. She has finally wakened from the early marriage life to realize that she is also a complete human being. She can do more than cooking, bearing children and keeping a house. She wrote that my sister-in-law had moved to town to guard her husband who was rumored of dancing with another girl. This is ridiculous. My brother went dancing? And, with another girl? Pooh, that was interesting. Anyhow, I am glad to know that my family is alive now. I'll write home. Mother's birthday is coming. God bless my family and me! Thanks.

December 15

Miriam rewarded me with a packet of flower seeds for the Chinese name I chose for her. I pray these Canadian seeds can bloom in my yard to let me remember Miriam and my tender feelings for her.

December 26

Clinton sent me a Christmas card from Burma. He graduated last year and is working in the south. My classmates were excited about this letter from another country. It was passed on from hand to hand. When it finally reached me, I found a red red rose beneath which was written: All things are subject unto love. I was shy about the rose but more shy about the words. So Clinton has not forgotten me no matter how badly I have treated him. I'll go to the library to see what a country Burma is.

Darkness is coming. Good night all the kind creatures! Thank

God for another day!

January 3

Harvey had warmed my bed for me. He locked the door from the outside when he left for his dorm. He would come early in the morning to let me out. He said this was safe though I had to do all my shitting tonight in the public WC. I laughed about his stupid idea. But he was serious.

I slept well, knowing Harvey would come to rescue his beauty from bladder swelling. Sure enough he knocked at the door happily while I was still sound asleep. He dreamt of a big fire in my room and I was dying inside. He was frightened and ran to open the door for me. I laughed while he was checking whether there was still some spark under my bed.

January 6

It has been snowing the whole day. It is bitingly cold.

January 10

Five days later I will be liberated from the anxiety of school life. I will be free to arrange my life in my own way. Think about it, more than ten years!

Harvey is not here. Only when I put my feet into the cold quilt do I realize how grateful I should have been when Harvey warmed my bed for me.

January 13

The first day was over. I ran all the way back after the Japanese exam and buried myself in Harvey's expecting arms. He lifted me up and swirled. He was happy for me when I boasted how easy the exam was.

I am making preparations for tomorrow. I hope time will never repeat itself when I am so spiritually strained and painful.

January 14

My vacation will start from tomorrow afternoon. Thank God for taking care of me through the four years peacefully. I did not go mad as I expected. I walked out of the exam place calmly. Thank Harvey who went through weal and woe with me.

O, the lovely kids at home! How I miss them!

January 15

Free at last! Thank almighty God, I am free at last! I had a walk by the bank with Harvey. Snow was melting. The air was fresh and chilly. Harvey warmed my hand in his pocket. He was like a kind mother, a lovely brother and a sweet little girl. The exam was over. Be it good or bad I was over with it. I had prayed hard and worked hard. I deserve a happy Spring Festival.

Chapter Fourteen

Farewell, My Dear Friend

January 2

I'm home now.

It's snowing. One of the many sows that Father raises is bearing piglets now. For the time being there are altogether nine tiny piglets. We put a cotton curtain to the pig sty. Dear old pig, are you in pain?

December 27(Lunar calendar)

Solar calendar crashes with Chinese Lunar calendar. The latter wins.

I have to switch my mind from scientific and rigid numbers to the numbers mother scratches on the wall. She can't read or write. Yet she is able to calculate the exact day when our old pigs produce piglets. She uses very primitive ways to remember things. She builds herself a whole different world without words. I used to ask her whether she was anxious in that world of hers. She would say what was the use of being anxious. Your grandparents were too poor to afford me even one day in school. Well, school was boring anyway. I preferred rambling in the fields and helping with the farm work. And she would start singing "Learn from Comrade Leifeng" at the top of her lung. This was one of the few songs she learned when picking cotton in the commune with other teenagers in the 1960s.

So I forget about solar calendar the third day at home. Lunar calendar means piglets, country fairs and the Spring Festival.

I went to call on my second sister yesterday. She told me about her love affairs with a young driver who parked his bus in the yard near her store. One day he walked up to her while she was washing clothes by the water tap and gave her a pair of gloves. The young driver saw my sister every day when he parked his bus. He said a man had to cultivate eight lives of goodness to be worth such a nice wife as my sister. He called my brother-in-law a big crook who fooled around with dancing girls and came home only once a month. My sister is terrified with such a love out of marriage. She is a dutiful daughter-in-law. What will happen if the young driver goes on like this? I sympathize with them. What about my story, the love I found and lost? I pray for Donna whose parents are against her relationship with her boyfriend Wang. I pray for my sister. I pray for Yangzi who is still dangling on the dead tree of Donald. I pray for myself. God, please enlighten us! I really hope I can do something for my sisters. There are so many things I can't take care of. Love will awake in the evening when I am alone with darkness. I wish God would take care of all the kind people for my gentle heart. Thanks.

December 29

It's half past twelve in the early morning of the Chinese New Year. I wish all the good people and all animals a happy, happy year in 2001. What will the year be like for me and my country? I'll install a telephone in my home; I'll learn the computer; I'll go to Beijing to touch the heart of China this year! Thank God for the passing and the coming!

January 1, 2001

I waited anxiously for Qin's coming. I knew she would come to see her parents and me. I knew she would be yelling my name and rubbing my hands happily when I ran out to meet her as we had been doing since the earliest days. To see her was as big occasion for me. I talked of her name when having breakfast this morning. My father sighed and was about to say something when he was sharply checked by mother. My heart sunk. What happened? I went to see Ping immediately after an uneasy breakfast. No, I couldn't see Ping. She was married to a man and went to another province with him. I was lost in the lonely lane. My two dearest playmates were far away from me. I sat on the old stone waiting for them while some younger girls came. How time flies! Qin, Ping and I used to fight for these little kids and fling them in the air merrily. Now they were about the age for marriage. They smiled at me and stopped chatting. I sensed something weird and asked them what they were talking about. After a short silence a thin girl said they were talking about Qin. What happened to her? My heart tightened and twisted. She killed herself. What?

What?!! I stood there dumfounded while the thin girl brattled on about my Qin's tragic suicide and lonely burial. Why? Why? I was too terrified to listen. I felt weak and sick. I walked toward Qin's yard slowly. I saw the old elm tree where I used to hide from Qin; I saw the old window through which I peeped in when Qin was having a high fever; I saw the yard where she fought with her brothers; I saw her mother who took my cold hand and let me cry hysterically for her lost daughter. She told me about Qin's poverty, about Qin's quarrel with her mother-in-law, about the poison farmers used to kill mice, about Qin's taking the poison in despair, about Qin's screaming little baby, about Qin's death, about her husband's broken heart, about Qin's mother-in-law taking poison too and about villagers digging a hole in the field and putting Qin in it......all came to me in one short sentence: Qin is no more! Suddenly, I hated Qin's parents for this fatal marriage. If her father hadn't squandered all the dowry money, Qin wouldn't have married into that family. If her mother was patient with her when Qin stayed with them after the quarrel, she wouldn't be so desperate. I hated poverty which had wrapped so many brave hearts with ice and cut young lives to pieces. I hated Qin who did not give me a chance to lessen her sorrow. I hated myself for losing such a friend as dear as my own flesh and blood. O, God, what shall I do? What can I do? No matter what I do, no matter how I cried in the toilet, no matter how I prayed, Qin is gone. She is no more. She has been with me for 22years and has left me now. Qin, where are you now? O, God, death is always so close.

January 3

I wish the rest days at home would go quickly. Something has changed in this village. I want to leave here.

What a life is waiting for me this year? Something great and meaningful, I hope. I will learn the computer, painting, guitar and earn my own living. If I fail the postgraduate exam, I will make a clear decision about my future. Maybe Lin will contact me. Maybe not. He's a stranger now. I can't find the love that inspired my life. What will happen? God, you are so tricky! It seems that I have to live my life patiently and carefully. Finally I find I am not in the mood for the festival. My mind is too deeply concerned about my future and my heart is too shocked at Qin's death.

Peace to the world!

January 6

Mother told me something funny about my cousin whose one eye was picked out by a hen when he was still a baby. He used to play with me before I went to school. He never goes to school and has been a laughing stock for a long time. I used to steal baozi for him and talk softly to him when others only shouted at him. He is five years older than me but still looks like a child. He used to peep at me when I came back from college but was scolded by his mother. I don't know what a part I have played in his innocent heart. I sympathize with him yet can do nothing to help him. He is old enough to set up a family but he is still a child mentally. I saw him laughing like an idiot with running kids around him when I came home this time. He always had a whip in hand, unleashing it energetically in the air while murmuring to himself. He seldom talked but he would grunt me a greeting when I come home. Mother said this cousin of mine had found himself a wife. Wow, what a surprise! He saw a woman sitting near a garbage can while he was collecting empty bottles. He bought her a cake stuffed with pork and took her home. At first my aunt was happy. She washed the dirty woman and let her sit on the bed. Mother was happy too. She discussed with my aunt and decided to check whether this mad woman still had the ability to produce babies. Suddenly the woman defecated on my aunt's new quilt. Well, she was mad indeed. My aunt boxed her ears and chased her away. My poor cousin pleaded with my aunt by saying that he would take care of his wife. He knelt down and begged my aunt to let the mad woman stay. He said he was old enough to have a wife. He wanted a family. However, my aunt's happiness and generosity were totally ruined by the shit on her new quilt. She closed her door to my cousin's "wife" anyway. I sighed after mother told me all about my cousin's adventure. What a pity! My heart weeps for all the people who lose their sense and become mad in normal eyes. I sympathize with the weak and the oppressed. I hope I know what I can do for them.

January 7

I went to see my eldest sister today. The simplicity of the old house and my sister's genuine love for me moved me greatly. I must strive on to improve her life. I am willing to live for the kind, the good-natured, the weak and the silent people. There is a kind of beauty in her gentle submission and contentment with the hard life. I pray for a better and deserved life for my sisters and their families. Qin took her life too cheaply. We live not only for ourselves but for the people who love us and also the people we love. This kind of love is deeply rooted in the general sympathy for a living creature that would end its play in real life sooner or later.

January 11

I am so worried about the result of the postgraduate exams. I can't sleep well. As soon as I close my eyes the exams would jump into my mind and I would be too excited to sleep. It's painful to wait for our futures to be decided.

A strong wind was blowing in the dark night. A kind of fear grabbed my heart. I screamed. Mother ran into my room to find me trembling under the quilt. She did not call me a coward this time but slept with me. Yet, I was ashamed. Why am I so afraid of darkness? Does darkness really conceal evil spirits?

January 14

Good morning! It is snowing!

Tomorrow will be the Lantern Festival. Many farmers have already put up red lanterns under their roofs. Evening comes. My dear countryside is alive with red lanterns and gentle snow. Qin, are you cold? Yes, you must be freezing in the wilderness. I should have burned some white paper for you. People believe white toilet paper can be converted into money in that world. If I believed this comforting custom, I should have folded you a thick quilt with paper and burned it. Yet, I did not. It's too tragic for me. I still want to see you alive. I want to believe that you can still smile to me. I still want you to ask me out and go dancing with me. Qin, how can you leave me like this? Keep well and wait for me.

Chapter Fifteen

Safe in My Heart

February15 (Solar calendar)

I am back at school now.

Harvey bought me a nice green diary as a Valentine's gift yesterday. I will write my memories carefully in it. I wish to grow up.

It's blowing dust now. I hate this kind of weather. I don't have a strong desire to prepare for the midterm exam nor a desire to learn. I need to make some changes. I need to see Lin and slap his face. Yet, I can't do it now. Maybe I need new clothes to cheer me up.

The last year in college means departure for us. Clinton graduated last year and is working abroad. Harvey will go to look for a job in the south. What about me? Will I pass the postgraduate exams and be a proud student in the Foreign Affairs College? I hope so.

February 17

We're having the final exam today. I don't care much about it. Now I know it's so easier for one to be deliciously lazy than working hard for an aim. Now I can sit by the desk and watch the sun rising and setting as long as I like. I can try every fantasy. Yet, I just don't feel as beautiful as when I was busy. My mind is like a blank sheet with a little tinges of sadness. I dream of Qin these days. It's so good to see her in my dreams. I miss her. Qin, how are you in that world? I miss you as much as you miss me. Your death makes me think more deeply about life. I can't think of you without tears. I wish God is kind to you there. I will pray for you.

February 22

The classroom is mostly empty after the exam. Only a few students come. I come to see the empty room every day, not knowing what to do with myself. Time passes so slowly. Sometimes I would draw the conclusion that I am not wanted by anyone. Harvey behaves quite differently this year. He doesn't really care for me very much when his own density is so uncertain. I am in a perfectly quiet state of mind. I am not pressed and sometimes I am not worried either. I am not eager for any change now. I just eat, read, sleep and live. Well, what else need I do?

February 27

Sunday afternoon was beautiful. Harvey and I watched the setting sun on the fifth floor of his teaching building. He taught me basic computer this afternoon. All of a sudden I got to know what a computer was and entered that wonderful world.

The girls are all trying makeup now. They want to look professional. I was the only one with natural eyebrows an hour ago. But now my brows have been trimmed too. No.3 plucked my wild and broad brows with a clipper. It pained. I looked in the mirror and felt weird with the trimmed thin brows. Ok, enough is enough. I must calm down to study now. It's stupid to rush here and there with the crowd. I am myself.

March 2

Four of my roommates went to another city to have an interview for a teacher's position. The remaining four of us sat in the dorm after lunch. We joked and laughed a lot. We are like a family. Then several months later we will have to part and walk our different ways. I am a little bit sad and tears are stinging my nose. These four years hold the most precious memories for me because I have quarreled a lot, laughed a lot and cried a lot in this tiny room. Yes, we will part. Every party has to end sometime. However, my dear sisters, I'll take you away with me in my tender memories. Wherever I go I will think of you and miss you as deeply as missing part of myself. Good luck to all my sisters!

March 4

The sun becomes more precious after the storm. I've finally come back to life again. Youth is like morning---idealistic, fresh and transient. I must have a high ideal. I've found there is much more beauty in striving forward than being idle. I mustn't miss the only chance that youth gives me.

Harvey came to show me his new suit. To be frank it was too big for him. Yet I couldn't tell him the truth for he was watching my eyes nervously. I smiled and said, "Aren't you a handsome guy in your grey suit!" He is happy now.

March 6

I am comfortable in old clothes though I long for a change. I went shopping two weeks ago but I was just not interested in anything. Maybe I was not in the mood for appearance.

It is still blowing very hard today. I begin to get tired of this dusty city.

March 7

We will take the Band 8 exam for the English majors today. As usual the students make a big fuss about it. That bad Monitor still wants to sit beside me so that he can steal my answers. Shit! No way!

March 8

My life will be drastically changed with the result of the postgraduate exams. My heart is so vast, empty and worried. Donna, Miriam and I went for an outing in the Cherry Valley. I lost myself in the gentle nature. How I wanted to melt with the sun, the wind, the trees and the earth! Cherry, when will you bloom? O, my life! My heart! God, let there be some changes!

March 9

I failed the postgraduate exams! I am also "hunting for a job"! I must be brave and confident!

March 10

I can't make fun of my life. I must have a plan. I must know what I want and do my best to get it. Harvey is too young and too simple for me. I shall always cherish the friendship but I can't promise anything more. Life is so contradictory.

I failed the exam. Foreign Affairs College has closed its door to me. Alas, a potential diplomat is nipped in bud. I lost my sense for a few moments on hearing the doomed news but am alive again. I can't give myself up.

March 11

Good morning, Pearl. You are still alive. Good!

Life can be more interesting if only I know how to perform well with its complicated plots. I mustn't be a nuisance to others and to myself. A strong and brave person will face the reality without losing one's heart. I've failed the exam. I can't and mustn't fail my life. I will not complain. I will not beg for help. I must use my own brains and hands to drag a disappointed Patricia out of the black hole. No one is in the position to help me. I must create opportunities for myself. I must feel good about myself again. Patricia, there is no God to blame if you fail. You must pick yourself up. Don't waste time! There is a much more beautiful scene in life than a success in exams. I can fail other people if I can't help, but I mustn't fail myself. Patricia, don't ask why; don't complain; don't close your eyes and pretend to be helpless. You must stand up again, and all by yourself. No one can give you a definite answer to your problems. This is life. You have to live it according to you way. You may be wrong or it might be the only right way but you will be always wrong if you are a coward and never try. Be brave and be yourself!

March 12

I got up early, had breakfast, put on my new jacket and new lip sticks and went to hunt for a job in the playground where a job fair would be held today. I squeezed my way in the crowds and presented my resumes to stern-faced bosses and came back to the dorm for a nap. Suddenly the phone rang. A college in Jiangxi asked me for an interview. So quick? I am not ready yet. I thanked him for the chance and told him I was not ready. Ready for what? I am not sure. But my heart would cry aloud if I give up the diplomat dream and be a teacher. I need time to coax myself.

March 14

Where am I now? In Harvey's home! We went climbing today and drew bamboo tablets to predict our fortune. It read I, Patricia, will be very lucky. Harvey was not happy with his fate. His tablet read he, Harvey, will be very unstable. I urged him to draw two more tablets which both predicted that Harvey would be very lucky. It was a fine day and I felt good on the top of the mountain and in the sky. I picked a bunch of peach blossoms and gave them to his mother as a gift.

March 15

I am back in the classroom again, tired, physically and mentally. I am in period. My legs are weak and so is my heart. I lost my student card and the original resume. God, what shall I do? How I wish to forget everything and could run away from the bleak reality! Yet, I have to move on. This is life. I can't stop.

Harvey is here with me. It's so good to look back and find Harvey is so near to me. I am a total failure. Maybe I need to be active but I AM tired! Who can encourage me? Who can give my life back to me?

March 17

I am empty. I have nothing interesting to do while my roommates are busy with interviews. There is a void in my heart that nothing can fill it up. I feel out of place everywhere. I want to talk with someone but Harvey is so obsessed with *How to Make a Great Fortune*. I count the days for wonders but nothing happens. Life is so meaningless and miserable. What can I do to add color to this pale picture of my last episode of college life? I want to be quiet and alone but am afraid of loneliness. It's only 10 p.m. but my mind is already numb. I must save myself.

March 22

A certain company in Canton asked me to have an interview next Tuesday. I found this plastic factory on line and sent them my resume yesterday. This morning a woman called and asked me to have an interview. What a change! I will buy some new clothes for the big occasion. I feel a little upset when I try to dress up to please others. Anyway the day will come and go. All this fuss will be over and I will be in my broken sports shoes again. I wish myself a comfortable journey.

March 26

It's the day for the adventure. God bless me.

Harvey saw me off at the station. I felt tight when Harvey left me alone on the train. Passengers from the south looked so different from the northerners. There was something barbaric in their eyes. One man stamped on my seat with his dirty shoes and yelled for his partners. A woman was smoking angrily while squeezing in the long queue for a sleeping berth ticket. Suddenly someone was crying that his mobile was stolen. I was like a lamb thrown to a group of wolves. I fought back the coming tears and called on my indomitable horse temper for help. I pushed that dirty foot off and stood up to fight for a sleeping berth ticket. When my turn came I searched my small wallet for two hundred more. I was embarrassed when the lookers on peeped into my empty purse. Finally I got the ticket and squeezed my way to the sleeping compartment triumphantly while some men whistled.

I was on the top bed. I climbed up and stretched on the small bed. It was my first time to be in a sleeping berth. My big body was not used to such confinement. I couldn't sit up straight or my head would be pushed into my body. I couldn't stretch my legs full or my feet would be out of the bed. So I lay on my stomach, elbowed myself up and watched passengers on the four beds below me. There was no smile on the train except the one from a little boy who was beneath me on the opposite bed.

Once the train started all passengers took out their food and began chewing. I reached into my bag and the first thing I touched was a can of apple juice Miriam gave me. Thank you, dear lady. Miriam not only gave me a can of juice and a bar of chocolate for the journey but also some suggestions on how to win the interview. She asked me some questions as the boss and was quite satisfied with my answers. "Miriam, what shall I do if I have a running nose suddenly?" I was quite concerned about my big nose. Miriam picked up a piece of toilet paper, wiped her nose while holding her head high and threw the paper in the dustbin casually. I laughed. So easy! What shall I do if I have a running nose? I wipe it!

It's five thirty now. God, what is the world like in the south of China? There is no one I can talk with so I talk to myself. What are my sisters doing in the dorm? Who are thinking of me?

It's 7 p.m. now. I must go down to have supper and have a good stretch. It's totally dark outside. What will happen tonight? The train is running through Hubei province now. The first stop is Wuchang where Chairman Mao fired his gun for the first time in the revolutionary history of China. We're passing the Yangtze River Bridge now. What a pity! I can see nothing in the darkness except for some flashing lights. China, how old are you and how large are you? Miriam, Harvey, Six....how I want to share this moment with you? Miriam, isn't it a miracle? We've come to like each other in spite of different language and cultural background. Thank God for this! I must be obedient to God, be good to people and life. It's 8 p.m. The train has stopped at Wuchang Station. I am already so far from my friends, my school and my city. Harvey, you bad boy, why don't you call the BP you gave me?

The broadcast has stopped. All is quiet for the night. Passengers are sleeping now. Someone is snorting soundly. What a big "dormitory"! It's 10 p.m. My sisters are going to bed now. Tonight they will find my bed empty and they will talk about me. Good night, the world!

March 27

Good morning, the south! Green, rich and wet Canton is drawing near. Thank God for the peaceful journey.

I am on the bus to Kaiping city which is in the suburb of Canton and is where the factory is located. The old man beside me keeps talking and talking in a strange language which sounds provoking enough to let me feel sick. It's drizzling outside now. Can I find the factory? Is this Canton? I see big red flowers, green and wet leaves, busy traffic and running people. I feel like I am in a different country.

Now, I am in the office of the factory. I've seen the HK boss and had lunch with the female employees. The boss looked nice until he offered me a low salary---1,000 Yuan per month. How am I going to live with such a low income in the expensive south? My heart sunk. He said he would have me trained in the

US for one year before I signed a five-year contract. I said I need to think about it and took the bus back to Canton. The boss was quite pleased with my professional clothes and braided ponytail. Yet, I was not pleased with his mean offer. I arrived at the Canton station in the late afternoon. Shall I go back to school or shall I have some adventure in the south now that I am out of Harvey's inspection? While I was thinking about this question---to go back or not to go back, a shadow flashed in front of me and ran away with my bag. I ran after him and yelled, "You son of a bitch, give me my bag!" I was furious. How dare he snatch my bag in broad daylight! Bad luck to him this time! I caught up with him, kicked his stupid ass and snatched my bag back. Without a word I walked into a nearby hotel. My legs were trembling when I paid the 300 Yuan fee and went up to my luxurious room. What if that man went to fetch his gang? Was he following me? It's rumored that Canton Station is controlled by several gangs who molest even kill weak passengers. It's the worst station in China. What shall I do? I peeped out of the window. No, no one was following me. I went downstairs and asked the guard of the hotel to guard me day and night. He looked at me up and down and said no one would bother a poor student. Well, good for me.

I went to my room and dialed a number that is almost rotten in my mind. He answered it. So he was lying when he told me he had lost his mobile. Lin was surprised to hear my voice. Was he embarrassed? How dare he lie to me that he changed this number? Was he happy to hear my voice again? I doubted it. He hung up after I told him why I was in Canton. I called again but the line was cut off. He did not care about me. The one I've cherished till my heart aches does not care about me at all. I smashed the phone and went to bed in this strange city.

March 28

I was woken up by the loud noise of trains and airplanes. I sat on the sill of the window and watched this energetic city. Planes fly so low. I can see their wings for the first time in my life. Cars sneak their way through the thick crowd. Trains whistle by, taking millions of peasant farmers away or bringing them in from all over China. My heart warms toward this vibrant city all of a sudden. Yes, I will accept the job. I will stay here and conquer this city. It seems that it can bring the worst as well as the best out of a person. Everyone is a fighter or an animal in this highly commercial and competitive city. Will I survive?

I jumped down from the window, went to the station and bought the ticket back to Zhengzhou. O, my slow, sweet Zhengzhou! My eyes sting at these two square Chinese characters " 郑州 ". My dear friends must be missing me. Three days' journey has opened my mind to another world.

March 29

The sun has risen up and is smiling at me outside the window. The girl and the boys beside me are still sleeping. They are all from the north. We chatted about the south last night which helped make the journey bearable. An old man got drunk and complained about the "beastly southerners" who robbed his wife and his money. He said it was Confucius who poisoned him. "Always choose the middle way! Be honest and kind! Give in to keep harmony! What's the good of all these rubbish in the south?" He had another mouthful of " 二锅头 " and wept. " 二锅头 " is the brand name of farmer's wine. It's cheap and strong and is a stimulus to sorrows and tears.

The sun is shining beautifully. I wanted to wake that drunk man up and let him share some warmth in the sun. I looked around and found he was still sound asleep under the seat. Poor old lamb, never lose your way among wolves again. If you are a disciple of Confucius, follow him to the end.

It's 10 a.m. now. Harvey must be waiting for me at Zhengzhou station. This makes the journey seems longer.

April 1

I need a passport if I really want that job. I will accept the training in the US and a five-year contract afterwards. I'll go to the public security office tomorrow and ask for an application form. Step by step I will enter another chapter of my life.

Is silence the best answer to a sacred love? I keep calling Lin and he keeps refusing to answer. God, you must help me. Let me love him without pain or let me forget him completely.

April 2

I've taken the first step to go abroad at last. I went to the public security office this morning and filled in a lot of forms. All these forms needed stamps from all kinds of authorities. I went here and there, begged, smiled and used my innocent tricks to have all the necessary red stamps banged on the forms. One woman was particularly interesting. She read the name of the factory and shrank away from the form as if "plastics" means "poison". She pursed her lips in a disgusted way and said she was busy. I went again in the afternoon and waited for hours in front of her office. At last she gave up, called me in, stamped the form and banged her door to me.

I'm still not sure whether to work in the south is the best choice for me. I am pushed by an invisible force. Miriam has found some material on feminism for me. I need to concentrate on thesis writing from tomorrow.

April 3

O my Gosh, my head is about to explode! The thesis keeps eating my nerve. I must have an outline now. What am I going to write? My head spins. Maybe I shouldn't go abroad. How quiet and comfortable it is to stay in school!

April 4

My brain doesn't work well recently. I get bored easily. I wish to settle down as soon as possible. The library is closed when we need it the most. I'll have to translate an article for my thesis. What a shame!

Nothing can ease my anxiety except time which is the very thing I hate to have now. I've passed so many ups and downs in my young life. I wish I could calm down to live a quiet and peaceful life. I'll wait. I am patient. I'll wait till another storm comes and goes. Maybe I should divert my attention to something else to drag me out of the terrible mess. I am almost bankrupt.

April 6

This afternoon I realized that Lin was wronged by me. I can understand him better now. It's unfair to compare him with Harvey who has no pressure now. If Lin were also a college student, he would spoil me more than Harvey does now. I still remember his experience as a construction worker living in the open field in cold winter. He told me this bitter past as soon as we knew each other which means he had trust in me. What can I do for him now? I still want to see him though I am trying so hard to forget him. I long for his tight and passionate hug. I want him to cry his pain out in my arms like a baby. He has the most tender and sensitive feelings under his strong mask.

April 8

To dial Lin's number has become a ritual for me. I don't expect him to answer it. He is too sacred to answer Patricia's phone. I just want a hope, a feeling that he is still there and I can still reach him. To my astonishment, his charming voice ran through the line this afternoon when I paid my homage to that number 13805885715. He is alive! I am alive, too! I was too nervous to talk, yet was so afraid to lose him again. I clung to the line silently and sobbed. He said, "You are not a child anymore. Don't cry. I miss you. I will go to see you next week" and hung up. I walked out of the phone booth with a tear-stricken face. Harvey was sad to see me sad. He did not ask me what happened but held my face in his warm hands and kissed away the tears. The more tender he kissed the more tears I cried. Who am I crying for, Lin, Harvey or myself? The intimacy between Harvey and I was curtailed by Lin's voice. I had to keep a secret from Harvey, knowing he couldn't have me even with all his unconditional love. I helped him build so many beautiful and thrilling dreams about our marriage, our home and our children. Now Lin said he missed me and I still need him so much. Yet, I am so afraid to see Lin, even afraid of thinking him. I have cherished Lin for such a long time yet he is still a stranger. I used to tell Harvey he was a stranger to me because I always kept Lin's face in my heart. However, last night when I looked at his face again, God, the face I had kissed and pinched and spitted on, it was as familiar as my own. When will Lin come? Will he come to see me? Forget it!

It is blowing dust again. God bless the world.

April 11

Fine day! Sunshine and mild wind! The Foreign Language Department will take all the graduates on an outing in the forest park.

I bought two bags of pickles with the only one Yuan I have and got on the bus with Six. She booked me to be her partner the whole day. We were like impatient monkeys, ready to make the forest upside down. I always fancy what would happen if I open another side of my character to Lin. I wish he could see me as a complete person instead of picturing me as a docile, naive and crying little girl. If I can be as spoiled and free with him as I am with Harvey, maybe it will be hard for Lin to leave me. I mustn't restrain my gorgeous light before his so called "mature man's civilization".

Here we were! We rushed out of the bus and ran wild in the forest; we danced to the chirping of birds and sang together with the running brooks; we chased blue butterflies and picked gold flowers; we played with the gentle breeze while swinging higher and higher……

April 12

I opened my eyes to find an empty dormitory. All my sisters were gone. I was left alone to sleep to death. I struggled up and called Lin's number. The phone rang and rang but no one answered. I buried my head in a basin of cold water and woke up. What are you doing, Pearl? You idiot, Lin won't come. He was lying. He has always been a big liar. He is nothing but a liar! He is a devil. Curse him! I must get out of the black hole. Six said, "Never fall down, for it is hard to stand up again". Other students are still pursuing their dreams vigorously while here am I, empty, miserable and caught in a hole. I'm eager to spread my wings and fly freely in the vast sky. Miriam said zoo was a sad thing. It's painful to see animals barred in cages. Here am I, caught in an invisible cage. I am as helpless as a mad tiger in a metal cage. It's strange that we have to wait for our lives to be arranged sometimes. I hate the Foreign Affairs College. I hate

Lin. They are the cages now. I must get out. I need to yell, to fight and to be proud of my freedom. I need to get busy to keep up with my restless soul. I'll write the thesis; I will paint; I will find a part-time job. It's dangerous to wait for my life to be arranged by destiny. I must harness it and be my own master. Yes, I need money. Why don't I earn it? I must be independent. When you intend to rely on others you're losing the freedom to do what you really want to do. I can't wait any longer. Harvey is not the one to inspire me. If we can't stay together, I won't blame myself for it. He is my pillow, my sweet boy, my dear friend but not someone who inspires me to dream great dreams. I hate commonness which I believe is stalemate. O, my God, I am still myself at last.

April 12

The day is ending. I am quiet, peaceful and silent. Lin won't come. I can feel the unbearable disappointment in the air. He won't come after two years' absence yet I have to go on with my dreams.

April 13

I clung to this Foreign Affairs College though my chance of being accepted was dim. I had always prayed for some miracle, hoping that the school would lower their standards and consider my scores. So I held my breath and called the school again today. A man answered the phone. He sounded so impatient that I was too scared to utter a word. Who am I to talk to the Very Important Person? Anyhow, I told him my score and asked him whether

I still had a chance to do my postgraduate work in his college. No. He said firmly with a snort and hung up. I wonder whether it pleased him to bully others. Well, give up this stupid dream! Say goodbye to school life and my na?ve dreams. I am an adult now. I will sign the contract with that plastic factory and go to the US to have the training. I'm eager to settle down. I am eager to do something else once I know this diplomatic dream is dead. At last I am liberated from school and I will catch up with the colorful and changing world outside.

I have waited so long yet no miracle comes. Let God be witness, Lin is not the right one for me. He is selfish and mean. He has only himself in his world. All he cares about is money, fame and face. He doesn't need sympathy so he despises love. He is a cruel animal in an agonizing China where old morals are giving way to competitive and selfish modern calculations. It's funny that I get such a conclusion after avoiding it for such a long time. I've always found excuses for his neglect of me. Enough is enough! I have to admit the truth and the truth is that he doesn't need to be cared for or loved.

April 14

It's a fine day. I went to the Bishagang Park with Harvey and had a warm nap in his lap. The sky was blue and pure. How I wanted to melt into the gentle nature and be gone!

A strong girl not only deals with difficulties but also deals with herself when necessary. I must overcome the feeling of decay. My heart should be as bright and shining as gold. Summer is coming. I should be active and happy.

April 19

The wind is roaring outside the window. What a Zhengzhou! What shall I do tonight? Yes, read *The Adventures of Sherlock Homes*. That factory in Kaiping sent me the contract yesterday. It was cold and business like. I did not know what else to add to this icy contract. I signed it and sold myself at a low price. Have I taken the wrong step? Five years later I need to go to Shanghai and be my own boss. Don't forget to get to where you belong. Running nose, no tissue. I need to go back to the dorm now.

April 22

I wandered into a Catholic church in a village this morning. Some farmers were singing mass. It happens to be Easter today. God, I wish you a happy day. Thank you for your love to the world.

I began to know what a chorus was. It was amazing to see even common countryside women could sing in an orderly way with their accent. What is religion? Is it all about God?

April 23

Nothing new comes to me. I am bored. April is almost ending yet I've done nothing that worth remembering. I need to take action; but how? I must keep my mind active and healthy. I want to go home to compose myself. I'm tired of worrying about bankruptcy and work. I'm tired of idleness. Harvey wants to go home with me. I don't know whether he will be welcomed or not. I still have no money. Maybe I can play, paint and be happy at home. I am able to paint sparrows, cranes, peacocks and all kinds of flowers now. Pray for something interesting to happen.

April 24

The eight girls in the dorm had our last lunch together. We wolfed down each dish as soon as it was put on the table and yelled for more. We were young, happy and somewhat desperate about the uncertain future after the graduation. We ate quickly to get numb. Then we had beer. Maybe we shouldn't worry about tomorrow. Tomorrow will take care of itself. A rich and sincere heart will save us all.

I still hope that Lin can come to see me for the last time though it is impossible. I CAN live a happy and useful life without him. I must.

The ferment spring, the sweet China roses, smiling sunshine---yes, I need to be happy though I've failed the postgraduate exams and my love has failed me.

April 28

Harvey has gone to his home and will go to my home three days later. I will go home tomorrow to prepare for this coming. I feel a little upset this afternoon. I've always been with Harvey and am so lost when he is not near me anymore. My roommates are mimicking the sound of animals to cheer me up. "Miao-miao-miao", "Wong-wongwong-wong" "hee-ang------hee-ang"......they are mischievous cats, dogs and donkeys. I laughed. Dear sisters, time has come for us to part. Alas, how sad am I!

April 29

I'm hungry but can't afford a breakfast. I will go home. Ben will see me off. Ben is happy now. He gets the highest score in a northern university and will further his master's degree on American Literature free of charge. I am sincerely happy for him.

April 30

I am home now. I long for Harvey's coming in solitude. How can I tell my parents he is the boy whom I may marry? How shall I tell them what a sweet boy he is? If I don't need money, all will be easy. But, I have to ask father for money again. God, I pray this is the last time.

There is really nothing to do at home. I am alone most of the time. I lose my appetite for food. I need an orderly life. My eldest sister came to see me and walked all the way to her home in another village in the afternoon. She is too poor to afford the one Yuan bus ticket. Mother urged her to pay for the piglets my sister bought from her last time. That was so mean. How can she say I ask for the money when I would give my own flesh to my sister? God, I hate you! Why can't I find a part-time job? I want to eat out of my own hands so desperately. Mother not only made my eldest sister guilty but also made my brother feel like killing himself. He has tried so hard yet money is always a problem. My coming home is like a nightmare for my family. Mother would curse anyone who can't give me some money. I am the scapegoat or the black sheep. How can I bear to see my sisters and brother guilty for not helping me? Their life is hard enough. Harvey will come tomorrow to hear my sorrow. I've told mother all about Harvey. She is not very enthusiastic about him, knowing he is as poor as me. Yet, Harvey promised to buy Yuan some new clothes with his scant money. He pities the little girl who still cries a lot. I need Harvey. He is not handsome but he listens to my pain and shares it with me. I don't want to hear any complaints against my brother any more. Now I can understand Lin better. He is like my brother in some way. They are making a living out of nothing.

May 4

Harvey is here. My two nieces are excited about a "foreign" visitor. They fetch him a stool and a bowl of hot water. They sit around him and stare happily at his smiling face. Mother thinks Harvey is too poor and too short and tries to keep me away from him. Poor Harvey! I want to go back to Zhengzhou.

May 6

I am in the dorm again. It's good to be back. I have to rewrite the thesis. I wonder whether I can write one all by myself but I don't have any materials. I'm terribly disappointed at the school authority. The library is closed. We are forced to cheat otherwise we have to fail the graduation paper. Maybe I am too extreme, yet how can I build a house with nothing? My own ideas on the Feminist Movement in the US? No idea at all! Zhengzhou is not a place to study. It's too advanced for us to sit quietly down to think and too backward to provide any useful information. What shall I write? What are my own ideas?

May 12

I'll finish the damned thesis today.

Six, Miriam and I went to the Cherry Valley yesterday. We had a marvelous time, looking for left-over cherries on top branches. When we say we are tired maybe we haven't worked much. If I can work happily, I won't be tired. When we say "relax", we don't just mean to stop working but stop worrying. I feel like flying aimlessly recently. God is dead.

Darkness is hovering down now. All is silent and sacred. I still have hope. There is still a thread of light in my world. I've experienced the most bitter test of a lifeless and hopeless youth. I've learned to cherish and to be cynical. I wish the sun of my dream still rises. I still need money very much but I will earn it. O, my God, why do you abandon me these days? You make me grow older than my age. You steal laughter, happiness and confidence from me. I am so afraid of the world. I am so afraid of human beings. I order myself to be patient and strong. The lesson I draw from these cold, dark and lonely days is to work, to eat, to do exercises and to sleep well. Look forward to a beautiful day.

May 16

I was still thinking of Lin's melancholy voice over the phone when Harvey asked me to have a walk with him by the Golden

River. At the sight of a short Harvey my prince charming changed to a frog suddenly. I was so annoyed at Harvey's coming that I threw his book into the river. He was just boasting about his most expensive book he bought the day before yesterday when I snatched it from his hand and flung it into the river. He was speechless for some moments then walked away but turned back to squeeze my shoulder hard.

May 19

At last Lin called.

He called when the roosters were crowing for the first time after midnight. I was wide awake, waiting and praying. Then the phone rang. It sounded so unreal and sinister. I held my breath and picked up the phone. It was him, the one who was killing me. I choked before saying anything. He said he was busy. He missed me every day and was about to hang up again. I controlled my emotion and asked him an honest question, "What do I do if I miss you?" He said, "Study hard." He did not know I was graduating. He did not ask about my future plans. He did not ask me where I would go after graduation. He did nothing but gave me a false hope and disappeared again.

I put down the phone and went to bed, too stupid to be awake.

May 20

It is 4 p.m. now. I am alone in the classroom. The blackboard has long been unused. A thin film of dust fell when I ran my hand on it. We had no more lectures after the final exam in March. Desks are empty. Gone are my classmates, hunting for jobs; gone are my 7 sisters in the dorm, hunting for a future. I am alone, so alone.

May 22

It's getting hotter and hotter.

I felt so down, so down that I wrote a letter to Lin. I don't know what will happen following this letter. I want to provoke him, to lose him and to be done with my silly heart.

June 1

Days come and go. I feel unnecessary to the world. I want to hide in a simple and quiet place where I can forget the passing of time. When I come back, all is done for me. Yet, nowhere can I go. Harvey is poor and busy. He can only go with me as far as the river. I must think of a way to escape the heavy and invisible emptiness. I am sick of the tardiness and repetition of routines.

June 5

A former PE teacher asked me to take a Japanese exam for a girl. The girl needs to pass 11 courses before she can get a diploma for higher self- education. She has failed Japanese twice and has only one chance left. I do not like cheating. But the PE teacher begged me.

I have to open the hideous Japanese book again and prepare for it.

June 6

I got the passport today.

I must make sure what I would need to apply for a visa.

June 8

I bought a silk green skirt today. Ready for USA!

I bought a pair of white pants for Harvey. He has found a job in Kelon, a big houseware factory in Canton. Maybe we will leave for the south together.

June 9

I am at Kaifeng now. Two hours later I will have another name and take the Japanese exam for that name. I feel betrayed, by myself. Kaifeng, the capital of Song Dynasty, was where the poker-faced general Baozheng observed justice for a decaying dynasty. His black face and fierce eyes sent a chill to the rotten bullies. He even cut the head off his beloved nephew when the latter was found guilty. His sister-in-law, who brought him up after the death of his parents and brother, begged him. No, the black-faced general was ruthless. He was the pillar of Song. He was a symbol of honest and justice. Yet, I cheated in this ancient city. I took the exam for another girl for 200 Yuan. I am so sorry general Bao. I need the money.

June 11

God, how can I thank you enough?

Lin called me this afternoon. I think of him all the time while

I am painting an eagle.

Miriam will leave China at the end of this semester. I don't know what gift is proper. Maybe something light and Chinese. Maybe my painting.

June 12

A new, wet and cool day.

I am still so happy. I am sure now Lin cares about me but something is missing. I am kinder to Harvey now, knowing we are definitely hopeless.

June 15

Rui came yesterday. My dear friend, my warrior, my sister! Ai, finally we come out well from college! We begged, borrowed, cried and finally, the four tough years are drawing to an end. I still remember the pain and humiliation on her mother's face when she went to borrow tuition for Rui from a relative and was chased out. The strong woman did not cry. Rui did. I did. Now, thank almighty God, the borrowing days are over. We could work to pay back the debt. Rui had found a job in Shanghai and came to say goodbye. Her feet were bleeding from high heeled sandals. I bought two bandages and covered her wounds. Then I walked her to the north gate. Trolley 101 came, taking Rui away. How I wished to hug her! No, Chinese don't hug. I turned and cried all the way to the dorm.

June 18

I am so happy. The wind, the setting sun and the clean sky, all look so clear and pretty after the storm. I am reading a novel in the classroom.

Suddenly, it poured, swift and hard. Students shouted and screamed excitedly. I jumped to the window and yelled. I love any sound from nature, especially the roar of wind and storm. I love the smell when rain is dripping into the earth.

I ran downstairs and was surprised to find Harvey in the rain. We walked across each other. I pretended not to see him and ran away like a little naughty girl. He was pretending to be a gentleman at first. When I ran, he turned and caught me. We laughed in the rain. It has been a long time since I was so happy. Yes, I like sound and change. The novel I was reading was also helpful. I feel alive when I can use my brain and imagination again.

I pray for an exciting tomorrow. We count the days to live our college life. God bless us.

June 21

All the graduates of the English Department will have a dinner together tomorrow evening. Time has come to leave. Happy leaving, then.

June 22

The dinner was not perfect. I broke down when I was singing a song named *"stay together forever"*. I threw the microphone to the floor and ran back to my seat, too excited to have a tiny bite. Then a fight started at the end of the hall. A girl was screaming hysterically and refused to be comforted. It was rumored that her boyfriend turned out to be a gay. He kissed another boy on the lip after a toast. There was sudden silence in the hall. We did not know what to do and looked at our instructor. To cheer us up, he performed a silly mini-drama by playing an old woman, a lamed man and a donkey all by himself. I was not amused. But it was very kind of him to try to please us. After the drama he toasted us and asked us not to forget the "mother college". Then we were dispersed.

Six and I walked together. We passed by Miriam's apartment. There was no light. She was asleep. We wanted to scratch at her door and frighten her up but were not sure of such a joke. Miriam is the first foreign teacher who treats us like friends. We like her a lot. Sometimes I think she is a Chinese.

June 23

Miriam, six and I had our last dinner together. Then we went to Miriam's to have beer. Six and her boyfriend Dragon bought a pair of antique vases for Miriam. I chose two of my best Chinese paintings as a gift. Miriam was packing, too.

Parting is everywhere.

June 25

Suddenly, I have the lingering feeling. I feel unspeakably sad. I don't know how I can see my roommate sisters off. The day will come soon for anther shore. O, the love we've sought here!

God, bless all my sisters and friends!

June 26

The factory in Kaiping asked me to write a statement to the American embassy to Beijing. I need to convince the officers that I would come back after 4 months' stay in their country. Why would I want to stay in the US? How could I prove my innocence? Why do I have to do that?

June 27

It's so hot these days. I can't sleep well and I get angry easily. God, let it rain quickly. I am so restless and irritated. Harvey has been rude and impatient to me these days. His heart has opened to the South. He is eager for new life, admitting it would be hard to remain true to me in that exotic city.

June 28

I returned all his pictures and all the gifts he bought for me since we met in that summer night. In the heat of central China I figured out that I don't really love Harvey. He packed and left for the south. I did not cry for him. My heart is almost rotten with a rotten name Lin. How long can I cling to it?

June 30

I get on the train for Kaiping. Yangzi saw me off at the railway station. She had begged me to stay. She asked me to read the old letters from Donald again and again till I was sick with his honeyed words and empty promises. How I want to shake her violently out of this stupid daze! Four years, she clung to this American man named Donald Steve. Why? Why? What's wrong with him? Or, what's wrong with her? Or what's wrong with me? Who am I to wake her up when I myself sound asleep!

The train pulls out of Zhengzhou. Bye-bye, the city, bye-bye, my college life, bye-bye…

College life is over. Innocent and fervent love for the other gender is gradually replaced by a broad love for all living creatures, men and women, children and the elderly, dogs and elephants, China roses and wild grass……Bye bye my little prince, you are the first one to wake me up from that short girlish sleeping . Bye the boy who used to stand by my window while I was too nervous to breathe properly; I almost forget your name now yet your green uniform and scarlet shirt shall live in my memory as freshly as the rising sun. Bye Jin. Your flying hair under the national flag, your waving arms, your loving eyes, oh, how they used to sweep my heart and soul. Yet, no more, all is gone with the passing of spring. Bye my dear Lin, where are you now? Not in my heart any more. I gave my heart to you on the grassland in a starry night and you tore it apart on that snowing morning. I used half of my youth to understand you, dream about you and love you yet you still chose to disappear into the crowd. Bye- bye my dearest Harvey, no one loved me as completely as you did yet I hurt you the most. I laughed at your shortness, made fun at your gentle heart and stamped on your broken shoes. Oh,

Harvey, tears can't rush away my guilt. You were too dear for me to torture yet I did. I lied to you, I cursed you, I looked down upon you and ran away from you. Bye, Harvey, I have to part from my own heart when I can't take care of it any more. Go to find a nice girl, Harvey. Marry a girl who is not wicked, nor greedy, nor as half bad as Patricia. I don't deserve your love. You treated me as a spoiled queen yet I chose to be a tramp. Bye-bye, my dearest love. Bye-bye all the boys I loved or dreamed or kissed. The innocent and passionate spring is over. Can you hear the gentle sound of falling petals? Yes, the once fresh petals drop one by one like my passing youth. Farewell , the one who touched my cheek in primary school while the whole class was flying paper planes; farewell, the one who roared while I was trying to be ladylike sensing his coming; farewell, the one who lay his head on folded arms and sang " my love is naked"; farewell, the one who whispered " marry me, my darling" while summer bugs were singing happily in the grass; farewell, the one who piggybacked me in the lonely summer night while I was crying on his back. Farewell, all my love. The petals of spring are falling. They have scented my youth, wetted my lips and touched my heart.

The End